Dissertations
in
American Economic History

This is a volume in the Arno Press collection

Dissertations in American Economic History

Advisory Editor
Stuart Bruchey

Research Associate
Eleanor Bruchey

See last pages of this volume for a complete list of titles.

THE ECONOMIC GROWTH OF SEVENTEENTH CENTURY NEW ENGLAND
A Measurement of Regional Income

Terry Lee Anderson

ARNO PRESS
A New York Times Company
New York – 1975

First publication in book form, Arno Press, 1975

DISSERTATIONS IN AMERICAN ECONOMIC HISTORY
ISBN for complete set: 0-405-07252-X
See last pages of this volume for titles.

Manufactured in the United States of America

Publisher's Note: The plates on pages 85, 133 and 134 were reproduced from the best available copies.

Library of Congress Cataloging in Publication Data

Anderson, Terry Lee, 1946-
The economic growth of seventeenth century New England.

(Dissertations in American economic history)
Originally presented as the author's thesis, University of Washington, 1972.
Bibliography: p.
1. New England--Economic conditions. 2. Income--New England--History. 3. Labor supply--New England--History. I. Title. II. Series.
HC107.A11A83 1975 330.9'74 75-2574
ISBN 0-405-07255-4

THE ECONOMIC GROWTH OF SEVENTEENTH CENTURY NEW ENGLAND:

A MEASUREMENT OF REGIONAL INCOME

by

Terry Lee Anderson

A dissertation submitted in partial fulfillment

of the requirements for the degree of

DOCTOR OF PHILOSOPHY

UNIVERSITY OF WASHINGTON

1972

University of Washington

Abstract

THE ECONOMIC GROWTH OF SEVENTEENTH CENTURY NEW ENGLAND:

A MEASUREMENT OF REGIONAL INCOME

By Terry Lee Anderson

Chairman of Supervisory Committee: Professor Robert Paul Thomas
Department of Economics

ABSTRACT

Measuring the progress of the American economy is a first step toward understanding the process of the economic growth. Many economic historians have devoted their time to this task but several gaps remain. Of all, perhaps the colonial period encompasses the largest void. The scarcity of data from the founding of Jamestown to the Revolution has forced economic historians to conjecture from the bits and pieces. As a result, there exists no systematic quantitative history of the colonial period.

The purpose of this dissertation is to provide such a study for seventeenth-century New England. The complexity of the economy of these northern colonies combined with the lack of quantitative evidence makes the task of measuring their economic performance most difficult. To overcome this it was necessary to develop an analytical framework which described the sectors of the economy and their relationship to one another and to research new and useful data necessary for measuring the region's income.

The first chapter of this disseration provides a chronological overview of the seventeenth-century New England economy. The second utilizes the tools of micro-economic theory to integrate the sectors of the economy into a simple general equilibrium model. Herein wages in the agricultural and resource sectors are linked to those in the shipping industry which are in turn related to English wages. Chapters three, four, and five examine the returns to labor, land, and capital from 1650 to 1709. To do so, it was necessary to estimate population and labor force on the basis of a stable population model. Wages are then combined with these estimates of the work force to yield labor's share of regional income. The shares for land and capital, however, are estimated from the random sample of estate inventories. Average asset holdings per probate are adjusted to approximate the average per living wealth holder. In the fifth chapter stock values of land and capital are converted to flows and added to the labor payments. The resulting income series is then compared with existing estimates for England and the colonies.

The contributions of this disseration are two fold. First it provides a theoretical model within which we can analyze the colonial New England economy. In addition to wage inferences, the model allows the development of testable hypotheses regarding the relative expansion of the various sectors. Perhaps more important, however, is the quantitative evidence developed to estimate regional income. The population estimates improve on existing figures and provide insight into the age-sex distribution of the inhabitants. From data taken from the probate records, we obtain information on the distribution of wealth holdings over time, the living standard enjoyed by the colonists, and the distribution of the labor force between sectors. The combination of payments to labor, land, and capital provide the first estimates of regional income for the seventeenth century. Growth rates inferred from these income figures suggest that the New England colonists were enjoying substantial intensive growth. Data contained in this work and the sources and methods used for its collection go a long way toward removing America's colonial experience from a "statistical dark age."

TABLE OF CONTENTS

LIST OF TABLES

LIST OF CHARTS

LIST OF FIGURES

LIST OF PLATES

ACKNOWLEDGEMENT

I owe many thanks to the people who have helped me in writing this dissertation. Special thanks goes to Robert Paul Thomas for his ideas, guidance, and criticism. My wife, Janet, provided the inspiration during the especially trying times. To all concerned I express my sincerest appreciation.

INTRODUCTION

Measuring the progress of the American economy is an important first step toward understanding the process of economic growth. Many economists and economic historians have devoted their time to this task, but a time series measuring national income is by no means complete. Since the development of national income techniques in the 1930's, the government has compiled vast amounts of data on the performance of the economy. Simon Kuznets, a leader in developing these techniques, has extended measures of national product back to 1869.[1] Robert Gallman in turn has expanded the income series to include portions of the antebellum period in American history.[2]

Efforts to further extend the income series back in time through the colonial period, however, have been frustrated by a scarcity of data. For later dates surviving price and quantity figures have enabled the estimation of aggregate output, but for the colonial era such information was rarely tabulated. As a result the time from the settlement of Jamestown to the American Revolution continues to encompass the largest gap in our knowledge of American economic growth.

Some speculation about the rate of economic growth prior to the American Revolution has been done on the basis of qualitative and indirect evidence. The interest in the pattern of colonial growth can perhaps be traced to Professor Goldsmith's testimony before the Joint Economic Committee in 1959 in which he points out:

> If the trend observed since 1839 had been in force before that date, average income per head in today's prices would have been about $145 in 1776, $80 in 1739, and less than $30 in 1676. It takes only a little consideration of the minimum requirements for keeping body and soul together, even in the simpler conditions prevailing in colonial America, to conclude that at present prices

> for individual commodities an average level of income below $200 is fairly well ruled out for 1776 or even the early 18th century. . . . There seems little doubt, then, that the average rate of growth of real income per head was much lower than 1-5/8 percent before 1829.[3]

George Rogers Taylor, using scraps of statistical data and qualitative evidence, offered the opinion that the eighteenth-century growth rate was one percent per annum.[4] Since Taylor's thought provoking article, other economic historians have placed the yearly colonial growth rate closer to 0.5 percent.[5]

The search for accurate estimates of colonial growth have continued but the results have been meager. Recent wealth studies by Alice Hanson Jones have provided quantitative evidence for 1774;[6] but cross-sectional studies of this sort provide little insight into the pattern of growth. Similar studies for earlier dates have not been forthcoming. As a result the colonial era remains in the shadow of a "statistical dark age." Without systematic studies of the colonial economy and new quantitative evidence, speculation and conjecture will continue as the bywords of colonial economic historians.

The purpose of this disseration is to remove such conjecture and shed new light on early American growth by measuring the regional income of seventeenth-century New England. The colonies of Massachusetts, Connecticut, New Hampshire and Rhode Island comprise about half the population of the North American colonies and offer a closely knit, multi-sector economy woven together by the commercial sector. The political area is large enough to provide a substantial cross-section of the colonial population, yet small enough to be handled within the confines of this study. Primary data sources are readily available and historical descriptions abound. It cannot, however, be argued that New England was necessarily typical or representative of the entire colonial experience; on the contrary her inhabitants were mostly Puritans, her economy quite diverse, and her climate and geography were harsh, all characteristics not found in other English colonies. Nonetheless, the income estimates contained herein do provide a basis for comparison and a foundation upon which we can eventually build colonial income accounts.

The complexity of the economy of the northern colonies combined with the dearth of quantitative evidence makes the task of measuring their economic performance challenging. This task can be approached from two directions. The method used most often in modern studies consists of totaling the value of all final goods and services produced by the economy. Alternatively, we can estimate aggregate production by summing the payments to all factors of production. Throughout the last half of the seventeenth century, the New Englanders produced resource intensive goods such as fish and lumber products, foodstuffs including horses, cattle, and grains, and provided shipping services to the Atlantic world. Since we lack price and quantity data necessary to measure the total value of these goods and services, I have approached regional income from the factor payment side. To facilitate this measurement it is necessary to develop an analytical framework which describes the sectors of the economy and relationship to one another. Within this context new data can be developed to estimate payments to labor, land, and capital.

The first chapter of this dissertation provides a chronological overview of the seventeenth-century New England economy. The discussion will focus upon the significant differences between the periods before, during and after the great Puritan migration. The second chapter utilizes the tools of micro-economic theory to integrate the sectors of the economy into a simple general equilibrium model. This model will develop the relationship between the final product markets and the major factors of production. Chapters three, four, and five will examine the returns to labor, land, and capital from 1650 to 1710. To do so it is first necessary to estimate population and labor force on the basis of a stable population model. Wages can then be combined with these estimates of the work force to yield labor's share of regional income. The shares of land and capital will, however, be estimated from the random sample of estate inventories. By adjusting the average asset holdings per probate we can approximate the average per living wealth holder. In the fifth chapter stock values of land and capital will be converted to flows and added to labor payments. The resulting income series and growth rates will then be placed in perspective by comparing them with existing estimates for England and the other colonies. Appendices A and B clarify the use of the stable population and present figures on the average size of completed family. Appendix C describes the sampling techniques used for this study, while Appendix D lists detailed wealth estimates obtained from the probate records. The consumer price index used to deflate all of the income estimates is developed in Appendix E.

Before proceeding two qualifications should be made. First, it must be remembered that these estimates represent only seventeenth-century New England. Since there is reason to expect differential growth rates between regions, caution should be used when making inferences about other areas and times. Second, as indicated in Appendix F, no claim is made that the figures in this work are free of error. Indeed, any quantitative study has potential bias; it can only be hoped that in this case sources of bias are at least recognized if not eliminated. The estimates of regional income found herein are the first of their type and should be challenged. Improvements in their quality can only contribute to our knowledge and understanding of America's past.

FOOTNOTES TO INTRODUCTION

1. Simon Kuznets, "Long-Term Changes in the National Income of the United States of America Since 1870," in Income and Wealth of the United States, Trends and Structure (Baltimore, 1952).

2. Robert E. Gallman, "Gross National Product in the United States, 1834-1909," Output, Employment, and Productivity in the United States After 1800 in Studies in Income and Wealth, Vol. 30 (New York: Columbia University Press, 1966);"Commodity Output, 1839-1899," Trends in the American Economy in the Nineteenth Century, in Studies in Income and Wealth, Vol. 24 (Princeton: Princeton University Press, 1960); and "Estimates of American National Product Made Before the Civil War," Economic Development and Cultural Change (April, 1961).

3. Hearings before the Joint Economic Committee, Part 2, Raymond Goldsmith, "Historical and Comparative Rates of Production, Prodictivity, and Prices," reprinted in Ralph Andreano, New Views on American Economic Development (Cambridge, Mass.: Schenkman Publishing Co., Inc., 1965), p. 355.

4. George Rogers Taylor, "American Growth Before 1840: An Exploratory Essay," JEH, XXIV, 4(Dec., 1964), p. 429.

5. See Ralph L. Andreano, New Views on American Economic Development, p. 50 and Robert E. Gallman, "The Pace and Pattern of American Economic Growth," in Davis, Easterlin, Parker, et al., American Economic Growth: An Economist's History of the United States (Hereafter referred

to as American Economic Growth) (New York: Harper & Row, 1972), p. 22.

6. Alice Hanson Jones, "Wealth Estimates for the American Middle Colonies, 1774," Economic Development and Cultural Change, XVIII, 4, Pt. 2 (July, 1970), (hereafter referred to as Jones, "Middle Colonies"), and "Wealth Estimates for the New England Colonies about 1770," JEH, XXXII, 1(March, 1972), pp. 98-127, (hereafter referred to as Jones, "New England Colonies").

CHAPTER I

THE SEVENTEENTH-CENTURY NEW ENGLAND ECONOMY

> "The wheat becomes flour and biscuit, the corn is made into meat, labor is converted into fish, and the whole is turned over in vessels of their own."
>
> William B. Weeden

A useful beginning for a study of the seventeenth-century economic growth of New England is a description of the forms of economic activity. Since other historians have provided us with several detailed accounts of both the overall economy and its specific industries,[1] I will present below only a survey of the main sectors of the economy, describing their inputs, location and relative importance within a chronological framework. Incorporated in this survey will be a discussion of the institutions and property rights which notably influenced the economic growth or the region. For the purposes of this discussion, it will be convenient to analyze the economy in two distinct periods with the break occurring near mid-century (1640) when the commercial sector first begins to florish.

Settlement and Expansion, 1620-1640

Long before permanent settlements dotted the shores of New England, European interest in the endowments of North America were obvious. Merchant adventurers in search of profits from fish, furs, and trade with the natives invested heavily in the chartered companies involved in economic activities in the New World. While the performance of these companies varies, it is clear that their involvement did produce much information about the New World, thus laying the foundation for future economic development. Out of this foundation grew many of the institutions which influenced New England's seventeenth-century economic growth. Since the early charter companies received their trade monopolies and rights to land from English sovereigns, an examination of the English government and its relationship to the colonial trading companies is essential to our understanding of the environment within which the New England economy operated.

To analyze the arrangement between the crown and private enterprise, I shall focus upon the fiscal aspect of the English mercantalistic system.[2] It is not the purpose of this discussion to explain why this particular relationship existed; rather we are interested in how it affected the institutional development of New England. Under this system the crown granted monopoly trading rights to chartered trading companies in return for revenues vital to the government's existence. These payments most often came in the form of loans, gifts, or taxes. From the state's point of view colonial development meant increased fiscal revenues; to the trading companies it meant monopoly profits from the resources of the New World. By collecting the revenues on the basis of company profits or from duties levied upon traded goods, the crown was able to greatly reduce its collection costs. Therefore, given the relatively poor administrative machinery of the state during the seventeenth century,[3] mercantilism was well suited to the ever present need for fiscal revenues. Initially, the English showed little interest in the internal workings of the companies and/or the colonies. As long as the financial statements of the chartered companies showed a profit, the interests of the monarch were satisfied. Under this situation the English government was more than willing to grant trade monopolies as well as political control over certain geographic areas outside the mother country. However, as the potential revenues from the New World settlements became more apparent, the crown did make some efforts to regain political control it had vested in the colonial commercial interests. In the words of George Louis Beer, "the movement toward greater imperial cohesion was wholly abortive. Instead of binding the colony more closely to the mother country, it resulted in preparations for resisting the authority of England."[4]

Under this merchantalistic system the English trading companies focused a great deal of attention upon the resources of New England. Initially, many of the expeditions were for the purpose of exploring, but the word of the abundant schools of fish found off the coast quickly attracted English adventurers. Fishing activities under the auspices of the Virginia Company, the Plymouth Company, and the London and Bristol Company produced ships loaded with valuable cargoes of fish from the northern coast. In 1614, the abundant resources of the region prompted Captain John Smith's Description of New England, wherein he stressed the importance of the fishery as the staple industry which would stimulate the economic growth of the region. However, during the early years, permanent settlement seemed unlikely. Although some expeditions did attempt to colonize such locations at St. George and Cupid's Cove, most English merchants were satisfied to victual fishing vessels for only the duration of one season. Hence, the European vessels would cross the Atlantic, fish off the New England coast; go ashore long enough to gather some food, clean, dry, and pack the catch, and trade with the Indians; and finally return home at the end of the season.

As these expeditions provided further knowledge of New England and as trade with the natives became more developed, permanent settlements began to dot the landscape. Viable settlements at Harbour Grace, Avalon, Winter Harbor, Damariscove, etc. had been established by the end of the second decade. Most such settlements continued to engage primarily in fishing and trade with the Indians, but sheer necessity required the production of some agricultural crops. "The merchants desired the emigrants to devote much of their time to commercial rather than agricultural activities,"[5] and in return agreed to supply the colonists with the necessary provisions. However, since many of the merchants did not carry out their part of the agreement and since migration into the region was increasing the demand for food, the agricultural sector gained a firm foothold by the 1620's.

The continued interest in the New England fishery, not surprisingly, resulted in a dispute over who had the monopoly right to fish. Sir Ferdinando Gorges, one of the most influential figures in the seventeenth-century development of New England, defended the rights of the Northern Virginia patentees against their southern neighbors. Gorges finally won the fight when, in June of 1621, a charter for the Council for New England granted to a group of forty men rights of fishing, trading, colonizing, and governing. With the founding of the Pilgrim colony at Plymouth, the Council's problems had started even before its charter was actually received. Throughout the decade various groups struggled for land patents and commercial rights, until in 1629 the Massachusetts Bay Company received royal charter covering the same jurisdiction as that of the Council for New England.

During the two decades between 1620 and 1640, seventeenth-century New England, unlike other areas of the English Empire, received its only large influx of emigrants. Of approximately 70,000 Englishmen leaving the mother country during this 20-year period, some 18,000 settled in New England.[6] While religious and social unrest on the east side of the Atlantic undoubtedly provided some incentive for migration, economic conditions were perhaps most influential.[7] Prior successful settlements throughout the New World greatly reduced the uncertainty of migration. Furthermore, differential factor prices between the two areas coupled with the profits to be earned in the mining of New England's natural resources added economic incentive for the move to America.

With this large influx of Europeans into the region, New England's coastal areas became well settled and her economy became more diversified. Building upon the staple export of fish, colonists began to exploit the fur and timber resources. Fur traders moved farther and farther inland searching for more profitable trade and paving the way for settlers to follow. By 1630 the permanent English settlements had forced the French and Dutch out of the coastal fur trade, leaving the interior of Massachusetts and Connecticut for the exploitation of English traders.[8] Permanent settlement and the expanding fur trade made known the economic possibilities of New England's resources. Especially in the northern areas of Maine and New Hampshire, the colonists turned toward the forests for their livelihood.[9] The exportation of timber, lumber, staves, naval stores, and even ships attracted an increasing number of inhabitants. Finally, the growing population provided a ready market for any surplus agricultural goods that might be produced. Initially, the colonists were to be supplied by English merchants, but as pointed out above, these merchants were often delinquent. Hence, necessity coupled with the profits available from selling agricultural products to newcomers explains

Darrett B. Rutman's paradox: "It (the paradox) is that of an agricultural land in which the trades of the sea are dominant; a land largely devoted to crops where -- if the tenor of historical writing is to be accepted -- profits are made in other endeavors."[10]

When the tide of migration stopped in 1640, a severe depression beset the Puritan Commonwealth. "The pressure that had dislodged Englishmen from their homes and sent them 3,000 miles to New England now found a new release in supporting the defiant Parliament and, eventually, the Civil War."[11] The continually expanding demand for agricultural goods in the thirties slackened while the produce available for market expanded, causing agricultural prices to plummet.[12] At the same time coastal fur trade came to a stand still. The receding beaver caused the emphasis of the trade to shift from Massachusetts Bay to the interior of Connecticut, thus substantially increasing the cost of obtaining fur-bearing animals.[13]

Since the early charters had vested many governing powers in the hands of the colonists, inhabitants of west side of the Atlantic were generally able to develop many of the institutions which governed their economic system. In the charters of the Plymouth and Massachusetts Bay Companies, for example, land was granted to the corporate groups for them to distribute as they pleased. While some of this land was retained by the company or granted in return for shares in the company, most was regranted to family groups which made up the units of local government.[14] In the case of the Pilgrims at Plymouth, land granted from the New England Council was originally held in common. However, by the spring of 1623 with the exception of the land held for common pasturage or for future expansion of the town, "inroads upon the communal land system were made without delay."[15] Home lots and the arable land were the first to be divided up and cultivated privately while the pasture woodland were the last to become private property.[16] The system of allotting the land varied greatly from town to town and certainly each had a different effect upon the distribution of income. From the efficiency standpoint, however, the important point is that private property rights over land raised the private rate of return towards the social rate thereby providing the incentive for efficient factor use. To be sure the property rights were not as well defined as they are today. In some cases common fields in New England continued to exist throughout the seventeenth century. Even though alienation was restrained by laws forbidding the sale of house and land without permission of other town inhabitants and quit-rents did exist, the New England colonies by the decade of the 1630's had made successive steps toward private ownership of agricultural land.[17]

That such arrangements did evolve in New England is not surprising in light of the existing governmental framework. As noted above, the corporate charters granted by the Crown in reality created political corporations with extensive powers of government. In most cases these charters gave to the inhabitants of the colony the right to establish legislative, executive, and judicial branches[18] within the guidelines of their grant. Under this structure the final authority for determining ownership of resources resided in the colonists themselves. From the viewpoint of the business organization interested in making profits from the monopoly rights on fishing, trapping, and trading, populating the land was crucial. Hence, "the individual grants which were made by the general court were usually in the nature of pensions, salaries, graditudes, or for the encouragement of some commercial enterprise" while community grants were for "the formation of new plantations."[19] To the receivers of these rights, exclusivity meant they could capture the returns from their efforts. In the words of Marshall Harris:

> "The corporate forms of government and settlement agency were crucial in the evolution of free land tenures of New England. No conflict existed between the holder of the power to govern and the holder of rights in land, and no conflict existed between either or both of these and the majority of the private landowners. This was possible because those powers, rights, and interests all resided in the same place -- the people."[20]

Due to high cost of enforcing exclusivity, resources for all intents and purposes were held in common. Monopoly rights were granted for fishing and fur trading and to this extent natural resources within the geographic confines of the grant might be considered privately owned. However, since the animals and fish were free to migrate to other areas, one had to harvest the resource as fast as possible or sacrifice it to his neighbors. Also, there is little evidence that the monopolies were rigidly enforced, for enforcement in the vast expanse of the New World where the Dutch and French traders were also interested in profits from the natural resources was very costly. New England forest land before mid seventeenth century were also commonly held for the use of all members of the town. Hence, all of New England's valuable natural resources were subject to the inefficiencies of the common property rights system.

Property rights in labor followed closely those in land, for as the villages abandoned communal farming, free individuals were allowed to reap all the benefits from their efforts. The returns to slave and indentured labor though not exclusive to the laboring individuals were the private property of the slave owner or the indenture's master. Like capital the only constraints upon the private rate of return to free labor came in the form of governmental regulation. Throughout the century the General Court made continual attempts at setting both wage and interest rates. Many colonial leaders blamed high wage rates and usury for failure of various projects but at the same time admitted that both capital and labor should receive "fair" rates of return.[21] Given the large number of buyers and sellers of the factors of production, competition in the market dictated the high factor prices. Hence, the efforts at control made by the General Court and by the several towns were "vain" and "fruitless."[22]

Under this system of property rights, New Englanders, during the twenty years following the Pilgrim landing at Plymouth, had made great efforts to develop industries such as fishing, lumbering, trading (including both furs and imports), farming, and even some home manufacturing. However, in spite of the early profits earned in these sectors, the economy was beginning to stagnate by 1640. To stimulate the commonwealth's economy several attempts were made to subsidize local manufacturing and discouraging imports. Nonetheless, despite these attempts by the leaders to make the economy self-sufficient, only overseas trade could supply the settlers with the goods they demanded and provide market for New England's staple products.

The Rise of Commerce, 1640-1709

The solution to the New England depression caused by the end of the Puritan migration and the resulting decline in the market for foodstuffs was twofold. If the colonists could find new customers for their existing products, exports would increase and their balance of payments problem would improve.

In addition to stimulating existing industries, a second solution involved a shift into the production of new goods or services for which seventeenth-century New England had a comparative advantage. The course of the economy after 1640 reflects both solutions.

The fifth decade of the seventeenth century marks the birth of New England's commercial sector which enabled the Puritans to find customers for their goods on all shores of the Atlantic as well as provide shipping services for both domestic and foreign products. In 1643 "no less than five New England vessels cleared port for the ocean routes."[23] By the turn of the century this number for Boston and Charleston alone had risen to a thousand,[24] while the total number of vessels registered with a home port in New England was 180.[25] New England's entry into the commercial sector was opposed by many of the Puritan leaders on the grounds that trade put men into a position to take unfair advantage of their fellows and hence destroyed the purity of men's souls. Despite these worries, the shipping sector expanded. The forests of northern New England provided some of the highest quality naval stores at the time.[26] Tall, straight pines for masts coupled with an abundant supply of lumber for the hulls made shipbuilding a natural industry. Sailors, able to man the ships, built and owned in New England, came from the existing and expanding fishing industry. The colonial fisheries says Weeden, "were training a maritime people destined to acquire wealth, and to make a navy which in due season might compete with the royal power upon the seas."[27] A combination of these ships and the trained sailors from the fishing sector provided New England with the necessary inputs for the successful production of shipping services. Corn beef, pork, masts, clapboards, pipe staves, fish, beaver, otter, and other commodities in addition to the staples from the Chesapeake and West Indies supplied the necessary commodities to fill the holds of the growing New England merchant fleet. New England's trade throughout the seventeenth century /was to the other colonies and most parts of Europe -- including Spain, France, and Holland. This commerce was indicative of her ability to compete in Atlantic as well as coastal shipping.

The course of the major industries -- fishing, timber, peltry, and agriculture -- which existed prior to 1640 varied after the flood of European immigration ceased. Since each of these industries employed natural resources in their production, we can shed a great deal of light on their relative expansion or contraction by examining the availability (supply) of the various resources. As noted earlier during the 1630's the colonists were only beginning to exploit their coastal fisheries which had been controlled mostly by the English and French fleets. From the first permanent settlements colonial leaders recognized the importance of their ocean staple. Certain islands were set aside solely for the purpose of fishing stations. Salt was exempted from most duties and men were often impressed to unload it when it arrived. Fishermen were granted plow lands and house and garden lots and in 1663 "were empowered to use wood from any common lands for fish flakes and stages."[28] By the middle of the seventeenth century, foreign interest in the New England fishing industry reached a peak and in 1661 the last English fishing vessel was said to have sailed for the New England banks.[29] At the same time, however, the increased use of slaves in the growing West Indies sugar industry stimulated the demand for New England's fish. With cod and bass still abundant in the rivers and harbors of Massachusetts, the fishing sector boomed. By the time of the Stuart Restoration, New England had complete control of her fishery which by 1708 had grown to include an estimated 300 fishing vessels. "Refuse cod" going to the West Indies and "merchantable cod fish" going mainly to Spain and the Wine Islands accounted for much of the bulk shipped via New England bottoms.[30]

Unlike the fishery, the New England fur trade had reached its peak by the fifth decade and experienced a relative decline throughout the remainder of the century. The beaver was not a very reproductive creature thus making the animals susceptible to extinction; that they were held as a common property resource provided the economic stimulus for their rapid exhaustion. Once the coastal supplies were depleted, the fur traders moved inland followed closely by farmers. Their quest for the legendary beaver meadows of the Great Lakes region were thwarted physiographically by the Appalachian Mountains and politically by the Dutch foothold on the Hudson River. In short, "the fur trade did not maintain its position of prime importance in the economy of New England for more than twenty or thirty years."[31]

The rapidly expanding commercial sector further stimulated the forest products industry of New England. Growing trade between all Atlantic ports produced a steady demand for ships which in turn brought masts, planks, and other naval stores out of the woods. Those stores not directly consumed by the New England shipbuilders were exported to the mother country. Also, the production of staves used in the construction of hogsheads increased as the demand for tobacco and sugar expanded. Commonly held forest land was quickly exploited making it necessary for the lumbermen to reach farther and farther inland for their resource. "By a law passed by the town in 1669, refusing permission to transport wood or timber by land or sea from the town commons, without leave of the selectmen, we can judge that a free use had been made of the native forest of Salem for lumber, staves, and ship building, as well as wood for the fishermen, and the common use of the town, and that the scarcity was beginning to be felt."[32] By the seventh or eighth decade diminishing returns had undoubtedly become severe enough to seriously impair the growth of the timber industry. In fact, as Weeden points out, by the final decade of the seventeenth century, naval stores in New England had diminished to the extent that they were imported from the Carolinas.[33]

For decades following the 1640 depression, New England farmers continued to prosper. Although the inflow of immigrants had ceased, thus shutting off an important market for foodstuffs, commercial links with the West Indies provided an entirely new demand for New England's agricultural commodities. In addition to supplying fish and corn to feed the sugar colonies' slave labor force, northern farmers began breeding horses for work in the sugar mills and for transport between the plantations and the docks. In 1645, two years before the beginning of large-scale trade with the Caribbean, an estimated 20,000 bushels of grain were exported from the commonwealth.[34] As long as land remained relatively abundant, agricultural output could expand with little increase in cost. Throughout the century as diminishing returns set in around the settled areas, families branched out and formed new towns; settlement patterns followed the major river valleys as farmers searched for fertile land located near cheap transportation to the markets. However, by the 1690's when the frontier had receded far into the interior, New England became a net importer of foodstuffs with some of the products coming from parts of the south and the majority coming from the rapidly expanding middle colonies.

By mid seventeenth century, it was clear that New England's economy was to be centered around her shipping sector and that many institutions had to be developed or changed to meet the needs of a commercial society. Since control of the Massachusetts Bay Company had been transferred from the Home Company to the General Court and the governor,[35] institutions which enforced and established property rights were much more responsive to the needs of the colonists. While international protection still came from the mother country, the growing local population increased the demand for internal protection as well as certain public goods. Governmental revenue was needed for the pay of the governor and officials; for the expenses of the General Court; for military expenditure; for construction and maintenance of churches and schools; and for the construction and repair of public roads, bridges, ferries, etc. To supply these services and provide institutions necessary for the efficient operation of the economy, the government and more specifically the General Court retained the right to levy taxes of various sorts. As time passed and trade flourished, the colonists followed the lead of the mother country and began to levy customs on certain commodities. Also the practice of licensing and selling of exclusive rights to traffic in specified products or localities brought revenues to the authorities.

As noted above the procurement of these taxes did involve the provision of some governmental services at both the colony and local levels. In addition to the enforcement of aforementioned property rights, during the last half of the century, the General Court turned toward the distribution of the increasingly scarce land to town groups and the settlement of boundary disputes between those towns.

The town proprietors in turn distributed the land amongst themselves and newcomers. At the local level property rights to animals kept in common herds were enforced on the basis of brands or earmarks; clear, permanent, legal titles were recorded; and common lands and the forests upon them were administered. The growth of commerce stimulated the need for the establishment and enforcement of rights within the market place. Decisions, such as the following, with respect to contracts were common: "All contracts in kind are to be satisfied in the kind contracted, or 'if in default of the very kind' they are settled in another commodity, then the damage is to be made up."[36] Of course, all sectors of the economy, commerce notwithstanding, were also subject to English laws. The importance of this charter provision became especially apparent with the Navigation Acts passed near mid seventeenth century. Even though the provisions of these acts, which required that colonial goods first seek English markets and pay certain duties to the Crown, were originally set forth in the charter, New England merchants continued to follow their own laws and sought free trade throughout the seventeenth century. By the end of that century, the New England colonists had long assumed the right to establish institutions and property rights which governed their lives, a fact which undoubtedly affected economic development during the era. A detailed study of these laws, customs, etc., though beyond the scope of the present work, would shed much light on the evolution of American institutional arrangements and their influence upon the economic efficiency of the system.

Summary

The seventeenth-century growth of New England saw a shift from an economy exporting resource intensive goods to one supplying shipping services to the major parts of the Atlantic world. From the early fishing expeditions to the Newfoundland banks, New England grew into permanent settlements exporting fish, furs, lumber products, and foodstuffs. During the first four decades of the century the population grew rapidly almost solely as a result of immigration from the mother country. With the end of the Puritan Migration in 1640 and the onset of diminishing returns in the resource intensive sectors, the inhabitants increasingly devoted their labor to commercial endeavors for which colonial New England is now famous. With these facts in mind, let us turn toward the development of an economic model within which we can analyze changes in the economy.

FOOTNOTES FOR CHAPTER I

1. For examples see William B. Weeden, Economic and Social History of New England: 1620-1789 (New York: Hillary House Publishers Ltd., 1963), in 2 volumes; Bernard Bailyn, The New England Merchants in the Seventeenth Century (New York: Harper & Row, 1955); Francis X. Moloney, The Fur Trade in New England 1620-1676 (Hamden, Conn.: Archon Books, 1967); Robert G. Albion, Forests and Sea Power (Cambridge, Mass.: Harvard University Press, 1926); Joseph J. Malone, Pine Trees and Politics (Seattle, Wash.: University of Washington Press, 1964); and Harold A. Innis, The Cod Fisheries (New Haven: Yale University Press, 1940).

2. See Eli F. Heckscher, Mercantilism (New York: The Macmillan Co., 1931), Vol. I, pp. 439-443.

3. See Heckscher, Vol. I, p. 454; W. R. Scott, The Constitution and Finance of English, Scottish and Irish Joint Stock Companies to 1720 (Cambridge: Cambridge University Press, 1912), Vol. I, pp. 448-463; and George Louis Beer, The Origins of the British Colonial System 1578-1660 (New York: Peter Smith, 1933), p. 370.

4. Beer, The Origins of the British Colonial System 1578-1660, Vol. I, p. 320. See also Weeden, Economic and Social History of New England, Vol. I, pp. 89-91.

5. Moloney, The Fur Trade, p. 19.

6. Carl Bridenbaugh, Vexed and Troubled Englishmen (New York: Oxford University Press, 1968), pp. 471-73.

7. Max Savelle, The Foundation of American Civilization (New York: Holt, Rinehart & Winston, 1942), p. 71 and James Truslow Adams, The Founding of New England (Boston: Little Brown, 1939), p. 90. Also this point will become more clear in the following chapter.

8. For a summary of the fur trade in New England, see Moloney, The Fur Trade, Chapter VII.

9. Charles E. Clark, The Eastern Frontier (New York: Alfred A. Knopf, 1970), Part I presents a good description of the economic endeavors of the northern areas.

10. Darrett B. Rutman, "Governor Winthrop's Garden Crop: The Significance of Agriculture in the Early Commerce of Massachusetts Bay," William and Mary Quarterly, 3rd Series, XX(July, 1963), p. 396.

11. Bailyn, New England Merchants, p. 46.

12. Ibid., pp. 46-49; Rutman, "Governor Winthrop's Garden Crop," pp. 397-400.

13. Even the fisheries, which prior to 1640 were controlled mostly by west-country and foreign vessels, faced some decline during the late 1630's. If the abundant New England catches were to be disposed of, in the future, foreign markets had to be exploited.

14. Marshall Harris, Origin of the Land Tenure System in the United States (Ames: Iowa State College Press, 1953), pp. 273-88.

15. Ibid., p. 274.

16. For a description of the administration of this common land, see Weeden, p. 275 and P. W. Bidwell and John I. Falconer, History of Agriculture in the Northern United States 1620-1860 (Washington, D.C.: Carnegie Institution of Washington, 1925), p. 23.

17. For the importance of this, see Steven N. S. Cheung, "The Structure of a Contract and the Theory of a Non-exclusive Resource," *Journal of Law and Economics*, XII (April 1970), pp. 49-70.

18. Darrett B. Rutman, *Winthrop's Boston Portrait of a Puritan Town, 1630-1649* (Chapel Hill: University of North Carolina Press, 1965), pp. 66-67.

19. Roy H. Akagi, *The Town Proprietors of the New England Colonies* (Philadelphia: Press of the University of Penn., 1924), pp. 9-10.

20. Harris, *Origin of Land Tenure*, p. 288.

21. See Joseph Dorfman, *The Economic Mind in American Civilization 1606-1865* (New York: Augustus M. Kelley Publishers, 1966), Vol. I, pp. 57-58.

22. Weeden, *Economic and Social History of New England*, Vol. 1, pp. 83 and 99.

23. Bailyn, *New England Merchants*, p. 83.

24. Innis, *The Cod Fisheries*, p. 119.

25. Bernard and Lotte Bailyn, *Massachusetts Shipping 1697-1714* (Cambridge, Mass.: The Belknap Press of Harvard University Press, 1959), p. 94.

26. Albion, *Forest and Sea Power*, pp. 234-35.

27. Weeden, *Economic and Social History of New England*, Vol. I, p. 245.

28. George F. Chever, "Some Remarks on the Commerce of Salem from 1626 to 1740 -- with a Sketch of Philip English -- a Merchant in Salem from about 1670 to about 1733-4," *Historical Collections of the Essex Institute*, I (July 1859), p. 89.

29. For a discussion of the reasons for the decline of the fishing efforts, see Innis, The Cod Fisheries, Chapter V.

30. Ibid., p. 116.

31. Moloney, The Fur Trade, p. 115.

32. Chever, "Some Remarks on the Commerce of Salem," p. 82.

33. Weeden, Economic and Social History of New England, Vol. 1, p. 366. The forest policy outlined by Malone in Pine Trees and Politics, pp. 10-27 suggests that masts and other naval stores were becoming more scarce.

34. Rutman, "Governor Winthrop's Garden Crop," p. 402.

35. Bailyn, New England Merchants, pp. 18-19.

36. Weeden, Economic and Social History of New England, Vol. 1, p. 194.

CHAPTER II

ANALYTICAL FRAMEWORK

By an early date in her seventeenth-century development, New England's economy consisted of several interwoven sectors. Puritan inhabitants, unlike their sister colonists to the south whose activities were dominated by tobacco production, cultivated the land for agricultural and forest products, the sea for fish, and the commercial markets for mercantile profits. Staple products were continually sought for trading purposes, but no single commodity shaped New England's economic profile throughout the entire seventeenth century. Farming, fishing, trapping, lumbering, shipping, and some manufacturing combined to form New England's diverse economic community.

The purpose here is to develop an analytical framework within which we can disentangle these inter-related sectors. By combining simplifying assumptions consistent with real world conditions and the tools of micro-economics, I will draw implications about the various sectors and their relationships to one another. The first step will be the specification of the production function for each industry. From this we will be able to isolate factors of production whose return must be included in the final measurement of regional income. Realizing that labor is the factor used by all industries, I will develop a simple general equilibrium model of the labor market.[1] In addition to implications about English wages relative to those in New England, this model provides a framework within which we can measure region's total product on the basis of factor returns. Again, we shall examine the economy in two distinct periods.

Agriculture and Resources, 1620-1640

Recalling the initial description of the economy, foodstuffs, furs, and the fish constituted the three main outputs of the society. Since the latter two commodities are produced by combining the same inputs, labor and resources, it is convenient to lump them into one sector labled resources. Hence, the New England economy between 1620 and 1640 can be characterized by two industries, agriculture and resources, whose assumed production functions are:

$$a = a(l, t),$$

$$r = r(l, nr),$$

where a, r, l, t, and nr are agricultural output, resource output, labor, land, and natural resources, respectively. During this early period it is assumed that the supply of land was perfectly elastic at some small but positive price. Although the cost of virgin land approached zero, the New England landscape with its dense forests and rocky soil required that the farmer invest much time in preparing raw land for production. This investment in agricultural land accrued a positive value. Likewise, during the early years of settlement, it can be assumed that non-exclusive resources such as beaver and fish were in perfectly elastic supply at a zero price. Hence, the prices of both inputs, p_l and p_{nr}, are taken as given by both sectors of economy. Under these conditions the demand functions for labor in the two sectors will be:

$$l_a^d = d_a(p_l, \bar{p}_t, D_a, F_a)$$

$$l_r^d = d_r(p_l, \bar{p}_{nr}, D_r, F_r)$$

where D_a and D_r represent the demand functions for the two industries and

F_a and F_r represent the production functions for the respective sectors. Following Chambers and Gordon, it is convenient to adopt "the convention that all production functions are linear and homogeneous if all factors are specified and all are divisible. When in fact a production function exhibits increasing or decreasing returns, it will be because of some indivisibility or because some factor is not included."[2] The constancy of returns under these fully specified demand functions and the fixed prices of cooperating factors are consistent with a perfectly elastic demand for labor in the two sectors. We must, however, examine D_a and D_r, the product demands for agriculture and resources.

Qualitative evidence for this era suggests that these industries did indeed face downward sloping demand curves for their products. In the case of agriculture, few foodstuffs were exported until after 1640. The Puritan migration brought newcomers who desired Indian corn, wheat, peas, and cattle. With local markets consuming all of the agricultural surplus, if all farms in the region attempted to expand, the larger output would entail depressing the price of agricultural goods.[3] Likewise, the fishermen whose cod were the major source of supply to England, the Mediterranian, and the West Indies could expect the price of fish to decline as they expanded their output. From an early date pelts from the New England forests flooded into the European markets. With their only major competition coming from the French and Dutch settlements in the New World, New England traders undoubtedly affected the European price of furs as they increased their harvest of animals. Since the industry demand curve for a productive factor incorporates these product price changes, the demand for labor in both agriculture and resources will be downward sloping.

Diagrammatically the labor curves for each sector and for the market are shown in Figure 1. For the agricultural sector where individuals maximize subject to the constraint of private property rights, the equilibrium conditions require that the wage rate equal the value of the marginal product ($W = MPP_1^a \cdot p_a$). Hence, in panel a I have plotted the VMP of labor in agriculture against the quantity of labor demanded. The constraint for resources is different for here one of the inputs is held in a common pool. Under this situation equilibrium will be attained when the value of the average product of labor in resources is equal to the wage rate ($W = APP_1^r \cdot p_r$).[4]

Figure 1

New England Labor Market 1620-1640

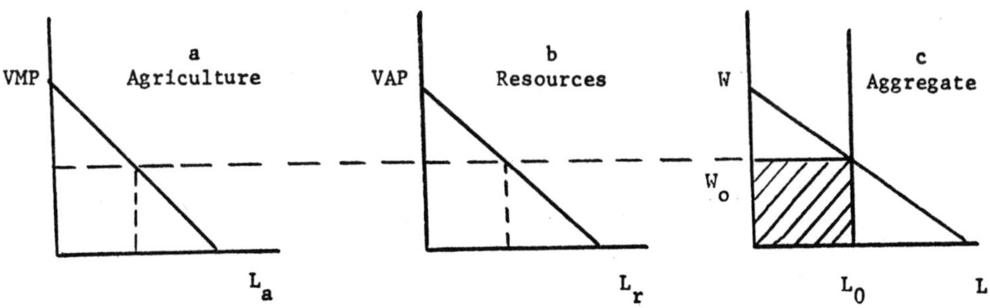

At this point all of the rents to the common pool resource will have been dissipated, leaving only a return to labor. That both sectors face downward sloping product demand curves is a sufficient condition for the negatively sloped labor demand curves shown in Figure 1, panels a and b. Assuming a perfectly inelastic supply of labor at a point in time, the aggregate labor market is shown in panel c with the total wage bill denoted by the shaded rectangle. Unfortunately, our historical records do not allow us to measure W_0 even if we could predict L_0.

The model does, however, allow us to predict the direction of change in the wage rate or the employment distribution given postulated shifts in demand and supply. During the two decades following the Pilgrim settlement, the demand for foodstuffs continually expanded as a result of the rapidly increasing white population and the trade with the Indians whose comparative advantage lie in fur trapping. At the same time furs and fish "always found a ready market"[5] in the expanding trade with Europe. Given the perfectly inelastic supply of labor we would expect the increasing demand for agricultural and resource commodities to drive up the wage rate. What happens to employment in the two sectors will depend upon the relative shifts in demand. Nonetheless, since the period in question encompasses the "Great Puritan Migration," the supply of labor certainly did not remain stationary. The expanding labor force would have dampened the upward pressure of the increasing demand and may have offset it altogether. That is to say, if the labor supply was increasing relative to demand, we would expect wages to fall and the rents of common pool resources to be dissipated between 1620 and 1640. Lacking actual wage rates, this hypothesis can be tested by examining the prices of output in the two sectors.

Examining the equilibrium condition that $W = p_x \cdot MPP^1_x$, it is clear that if there are no diminishing returns trends the final product price will mirror the wage rate. While New England price data for this early period is quite scarce, the evidence does suggest a downward trend in the relative price of agricultural and resource commodities.[6] This evidence combined with the well-documented depression of the late 1630's[7] suggests that prices and hence wages were indeed falling. We cannot refute the hypothesis that the supply of labor was expanding relative to the demand.

Before turning to the post 1640 New England economy, one final point should be made about the absolute level of wages between 1620 and 1640. Historians have always considered the wages and economic conditions in the New World to be an important factor in attracting migrants. Says Weeden, "the majority of these men and women (referring to the Pilgrims) left home and braved terrors of sea and wilderness to better their condition economically and socially."[8] No matter what other motives may have induced any one, from John Cabot to the last arrival at Ellis Island, to turn his face westward, added to them has ever been the hope of bettering his economic condition."[9] In other words, it is generally believed that wages in the Puritan commonwealth were above the wages available to the newcomers had they remained in England. The continued migration until the early 1640's is certainly consistent with this belief. However, since the majority of the immigrants were Puritans who were "alledgedly" discriminated against in the mother country, there is some question as to whether or not their alternative English wage or opportunity cost was below the average English wage. If it was below, it is possible for the New World wage, W_0, to be below the English average but above the Puritan average thus still providing incentive for Puritan migration. We can add theoretical support to long-standing belief that New World wages were above the average of those in the Old. Assuming they were maximizing individuals, once in New England the Puritans would choose occupations which yielded the highest return. The choice of agriculture and resources therefore suggests that these endeavors were the highest valued options. If in choosing these occupations the colonist forewent alternatives paying a wage equal to the averages of those in England, we can conclude that early colonial wages were indeed above those in the mother country. This was the case in New England prior to 1640, for during this period the colonists did not enter the shipping sector which, as we shall see in the next section, paid wages at least equal to those in England. The equilibrium wage before the fifth decade of the seventeenth century must have exceeded the English average.

Rise of Commerce, 1640-1709

The meager wage and price evidence of the 1630's combined with the well-documented depression of 1640 suggests that for the twenty years following Pilgrim settlement, the supply of labor was increasing relative to demand. In addition to the fur trade, early settlers enjoyed prosperity from the sale of agricultural surplus to new materials. While the increased migration during the forth decade did in fact stimulate the demand for agricultural commodities, the increments to the labor force likewise added to the available supply of goods. The tide of religious descenters undoubtedly ebbed partly as the result of the Puritan Revolution which raised the prospects for a better life in England. But the "pull stimulus" on the west side of the Atlantic also had its influence. That in 1640 "there were many sellers, few buyers, and hardly any currency"[10] implies economic conditions had changed. The early years of prosperity with their high prices and wages were gone.

Recalling the earlier description of the mid-seventeenth-century economy, the depression of the 40's marked New England's entry into the growing Atlantic trade. As a newcomer in the Atlantic trade, New England entered into direct competition with the English shipping industry. Given this competition in the Atlantic shipping market, let us consider the demand for labor by the New England commercial sector, the output of which was a function of labor and capital, $c = c(l, k)$.

The elasticity of demand for labor in this sector will be determined by the elasticity of supply of the other factor, the elasticity of demand for the final product, and the production conditions for the firms within the industry. For our purposes we can take the supply of capital as perfectly elastic. "The merchants who migrated to Massachusetts kept their connections in the mother country, and even added new ones, especially those anxious to gain a foothold in a new market with potential."[11] During the entire century New England was only a small consumer in the market for world capital. Hence, at a point in time the price of capital, p_k, can be assumed constant at the world price, i.e., increases in demand by the colonists will not affect this price. The demand curve for labor can now be expressed as,

$$l_c^d = d_c(p_l, \bar{p}_k, D_c, F_c).$$

Further, since New England supplied only a small portion of the total seventeenth-century shipping services, changes in the quantity she produced would not substantially affect the competitive price of those services. New England was a price taker facing a perfectly elastic demand for her commercial services. Retaining the assumption that the production function for this sector exhibits first degree homogeneity produces the result that the demand for labor in the commercial sector, l_c^d, is perfectly elastic.[12]

Combining the demand for labor in the commercial sector with that of the already existing sectors produces a simple three-sector general equilibrium model for the New England labor market. It is assumed that by the 1640's rents

Figure 2

New England Labor Market 1640-1710

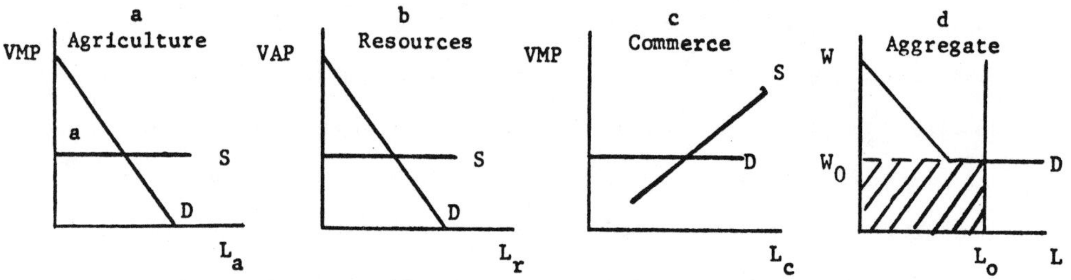

in the resource sector had been dissipated so that factor returns in the economy consisted of wages (shaded rectangle), land rents (triangle a), and capital payments (not shown). As can be seen in Figure 2, the significant change from the pre-1640 model is in the aggregate labor market where the demand curve now has a perfectly elastic portion. As long as any individuals remain employed in the commercial sector, the supply of labor to the initial two sectors will be perfectly elastic at the wage rate in shipping. Moreover, the average wage in New England will be determined in the commercial sector. The supply of labor to commerce is derived by asking how much labor will be demanded by the agricultural and resource sectors at alternative wages and subtracting that amount from the total quantity of labor available. In this manner the shipping sector becomes the residual receiver of labor, i.e., ceterds paribus any increase in the aggregate labor force will be absorbed into the commercial sector with no increase in the average wage. Furthermore, upward shifts in the demand for labor in this sector will necessarily cause contraction of the other two sectors. Within the framework of this model, comparisons of the distribution of the labor force over time will enable us to make statements about demand shifts in the various sectors.

Although wage data for post-1640 New England is little improved over the earlier period, the rise of the commercial sector does allow direct comparison with the English labor market. As established above the wage rate, W_0, shown in Figure 2, panel d, is determined by the value of the marginal product in the shipping industry where $w_c = MPP_1^c \cdot p_c$. Let us compare these components of the mid-seventeenth-century wage rate with those in England, beginning with p_c or the freight rate.

From the earliest date of her shipping ventures, New England merchants competed with vessels from the mother country. Ralph Davis in his authorative study of English shipping alluded to this competition:

> New England was the home of American shipbuilding industry, and American ships soon began to carry a considerable part of the limited volume of trade that was available. The real importance of New England to this study lies not in the subject dealt with here -- the demands of trade on the English shipping industry -- but in its role (though a surprisingly small one) as a competitor in other branches of transatlantic traffic. . . .[13]

The other branches to which Davis refers include Spain, France, Portugal, and African coast, but the valuable West Indian trade was perhaps the most important. By the end of the seventeenth century, New England based vessels dominated the coastal trade of North America, but the English were not entirely absent. By the middle of the following century colonial merchants had even come to dominate the route between New England soil and the mother country, with the number of colonial and British owned entries being 68 and 32 and clearances 85 and 15 respectively.[14] With these crown and colonial ships traveling the same routes, competing for the same "limited volume of trade," we would expect them to receive the same price for their services. On this basis it is assumed that p_c is the same for industries on both sides of the Atlantic.

Moreover, productivity differed little if any between British and colonial sailors. Many New England seamen received their training in the English navy and many others learned the skills of the sea while working in the prosperous New England fishing industry.[15] The ships or capital likewise was of same quality in Old or New England. Many of the seventeenth-century hulls were in fact built in New England shipyards and sold to English merchants.[16] Once produced shipping technology whether embodied in labor or capital was a free good transferable between the firms competing to supply commercial services. Hence, it is reasonable to assume that the marginal physical product of labor, MPP_1^c, was equal on all English bottoms regardless of their port of origin.

Given the competition between New and Old English commercial enterprises, I have assumed that English seamen's wages are a good proxy for those in the Puritan commonwealth during the last half of the seventeenth century. _Ceteris paribus_, if one sector had been able to secure labor at a lower price, they would have driven their competitors out of the market. This conclusion is consistent with the historical evidence presented in Table II-1. Via the linking commercial sectors, English wages do provide evidence of the general trend in New England wages where the original data is lacking.

TABLE II-1

COMPARISON OF SEAMEN'S MONTHLY WAGES IN ENGLAND AND NEW ENGLAND

	Peace		War	
Job	New England[1]	England[2]	New England[3]	England[4]
Master	120 s.	120 s.	120 s.	120 s.
Chief Mate	80 s.	78 s.	90 s.	90 s.
Sailor	35-55 s.	39 s.	60-75 s.	72 s.

[1]Weedon, Economic and Social History of New England, p. 269.

[2]Davis, The Rise of the English Shipping Industry, pp. 138-140. For chief mate I averaged the wages listed. For sailors I averaged the wages of all other men on abroad.

[3]Weedon, p. 887.

[4]Davis, pp. 138-140.

Summary

During the early settlement of New England quasi rents were earned by newcomers from the mother country but as these rents attracted immigrants, the supply of labor shifted relative to the demand and the average wage was driven toward the alternative English wage. This continuous downward pressure coupled with political conditions in England halted the flow of migration early in the fifth decade. Faced with the prospect of even lower wages as natural propagation increased the labor force, the Yankee inhabitants had the choice of returning home or finding an industry with a value of marginal product (wage) compared to that in England. Although some undoubtedly chose to migrate,[17] many entered the rapidly growing commercial sector. By combining their labor with capital and competing for the Atlantic trade, New Englanders were able to earn wages equal to those of the English sailors. Since this competition persisted throughout the seventeenth century, there was no room for differential wages and hence no incentive for migration between the two areas. Changes in the average wage rate could only occur as the result of a shift in the demand for labor in commerce. Moreover, changes in the distribution of the labor force between the occupations depended upon demand shifts in the export oriented agriculture and resource sectors. Quite simply, New England had become the tail on a large dog commonly known as the English mercantile empire.

In this chapter I have presented a framework within which we can measure regional income from the factor payments. An examination of the economy near the middle of the seventeenth century revealed three major sectors, agriculture, resources, and commerce. For the purpose of the model described above, it was assumed that the output of these sectors was a function of labor and land, labor and natural resources, and labor and capital, respectively. The theoretical implications of the model justify the use of English wages as a proxy for the rate of return to New England labor. It should be realized, however, that the simplifying assumptions of the model omit capital from both the agricultural and resource sectors. While this omission does not affect the results of the model with respect to labor, payments to capital in all endeavors must be included in the final estimate of regional income. Hence, in the reamining chapters we will compute the labor force and its income and add to that the discounted value of the land and capital stock to arrive at estimates of New England's aggregate and per capita incomes from 1650 to 1709.

FOOTNOTES FOR CHAPTER II

1. The model is similar to the one employed by Chambers and Gordon to analyze the twentieth-century Canadian wheat boom. See Edward J. Chambers and Donald F. Gordon, "Primary Products and Economic Growth: An Empirical Measurement," Journal of Political Economy, LXXIV, (August 1966), pp. 315-332.

2. Ibid., p. 318.

3. Rutman, "Governor Winthrop's Garden Crop," p. 399.

4. For a complete discussion of the equilibrium conditions with common property rights, see H. Scott Gordon, "The Economic Theory of a Common Property Resource: The Fishery," Journal of Political Economy, 62 (1954). The dissipation of rents under this situation is described by Cheung, "The Structure of a Contract."

5. Moloney, The Fur Trade, p. 16.

6. Weeden, Economic and Social History of New England, Vol. II, Appendix A.

7. Rutman, "Governor Winthrop's Garden Crop," p. 398.

8. Weeden, Economic and Social History of New England, Vol. I, p. 15.

9. Adams, The Founding of New England, p. 90.

10. Weeden, Economic and Social History of New England, Vol. 1, p. 165.

11. For a discussion of capital markets and how they operated in the absence of a large international banking network, see Bailyn, New England Merchants, pp. 88-89; William S. Sachs and Ari Hoogenboom, The Enterprising

Colonials (Chicago: Argonaut, Inc., Publishers, 1965), p. 9; Weeden, Economic and Social History of New England, Vol. I, p. 256; and Innis, The Cod Fisheries, pp. 133-34.

12. The linear and homogeneous production function implies that output increases by the same proportion for the range of input combinations under consideration. The fact that over the century many ships of varying size competed on the same routes supports this assumption since any trend toward increasing or decreasing returns would have been reflected in the use of larger or smaller vessels. See Douglass C. North, "Sources of Productivity Change in Ocean Shipping, 1600-1850," Journal of Political Economy, 76 (September/October 1968), p. 958.

13. Ralph Davis, The Rise of English Shipping Industry (London: St. Martin's Press, 1962), pp. 290-291. For further descriptions of New England's participation in Atlantic trade, see Bailyn, New England Merchants, Chapter IV.

14. Shepard and Walton, Shipping, Maritime Trade, and the Economic Development, Chapter II.

15. Weeden, Economic and Social History of New England, Vol. I, p. 245, and Innis, The Cod Fisheries, p. 137.

16. Weeden, Vol. I, pp. 365-66.

17. See James Kendal Hosmer, ed., Winthrop's Journal "History of New England," 1630-1649 (New York, 1908), Vol. I, pp. 333-335 and Vol. II, pp. 11, 33-34, 207.

CHAPTER III

POPULATION, LABOR FORCE AND PAYMENTS TO LABOR

When estimating the regional income via the factor payment method, the payment to labor, even in the highly industrialized modern economies always constitutes the bulk of the income. Hence what happens to the size and rate of compensation of the labor force is crucial to any economic history. To measure this compensation for seventeenth-century New England, it is necessary to estimate both the quantity of labor employed and the wage rate. In light of the analytical framework presented in chapter II, it is possible to estimate the rate of compensation despite the dearth of New England data. However, it still remains to establish reliable population and labor force figures for this century.

The economic and social history of the American colonies has recently -- after more than two generations of comparative neglect -- been the subject of a new wave of research. This burst of investigative energy is mainly due to the development of an interest in quantitative history and the re-discovery of many primary sources that lend themselves to quantitative analysis. Most of the research of the "new" history has been confined to the processing of the quantitative materials and the drawing of direct inferences. Such inferences have provided a wealth of new demographic information on such things as life expectancy, age of marriage, maternity frequency, etc.[1] Unfortunately, until now no research has attempted to combine this knowledge into a systematic demographic study of the pattern of seventeenth-century New England population growth.

The purpose of this chapter is to provide the missing link between the population parameters and the aggregate estimates and combine the resulting labor force estimates with the proxy wage rate. Below I will first critically review the existing population series for colonial New England. Following this, I will discuss and apply a stable model to the conditions existing in New England, present the findings on the average size of completed family, and derive estimates of the natural rate of increase of the population. This natural rate of increase plus an estimate of the base population allows the construction of a decade series. After checking the prediction of 1690 against independent evidence, a calculation of the labor force on the basis of the age-sex distribution of the population will be made. By examining various English wage rates and multiplying them times the labor force, I will arrive at the chapter's final product, seventeenth-century labor payments.

Review of Existing Estimates

There have been several attempts to estimate the population of colonial America, two of which deserve our attention because of their completeness and wide acceptance. The first of these to appear was that of W. S. Rossiter, Chief Clerk of the Bureau of the Census.[2] Rossiter's estimates which are broken down by colony appear to rely heavily upon the previous researches of Franklin Dexter.[3] Subsequent to Rossiter's series Stella Sutherland has published in *Historical Statistics* another complete series of decade estimates by colony of the population of the thirteen American colonies that later formed the United States.[4] Sutherland's estimates appear to be a detailed revision of the Rossiter series utilizing new evidence that has come to light in the more than forty years that separate the two series. Sutherland's series is more detailed than Rossiter's in that it contains a separate estimate by colony and decade of the black population.

If Sutherland's estimates of the black population in New England are subtracted from both Rossiter's and Sutherland's total New England population, it becomes possible to compare the two series with respect to only the white population. It is noteworthy that before 1700 Blacks represent only a small portion of the total New England population. A galnce at the two series, shown in Table I, indicates that the two series are quite dissimilar, both in the absolute magnitudes of the decade estimates and in the rates of growth exhibited between decades. Thus an economic historian will find any explanation of the growth or development of the New England economy based upon population seriously affected by his choice of estimates.

The differences are striking, if perhaps understandable. The Sutherland series as a percentage of Rossiter's by decade is shown in Column 4 of Table I. Between 1650 and 1700 it ranges from .83 of Rossiter's in 1650 to 1.4 in 1670. The rate of growth of the population between decades also shows wide variation. Sutherland's series, for example, exhibits decade growth rates from 66.5 percent in 1640's and 58.3 percent in the 1660's to only 5.9 percent between 1690 and 1700. Such large swings suggest to the historical demographer that immigration, emigration and/or major catastrophies must have played a large role in determining the population of colonial New England in the seventeenth century. Rossiter's estimates on the other hand vary much less, averaging a growth rate of 31.3 percent per decade.

Below we shall point out that implicitly the two series seem to reflect radically different views of the demographic factors that controlled the rate of growth of the New England white population. However, the nature of the evidence and the methods employed by both can perhaps account for much of their dissimilarity. The evidence upon which the two series rest are the surviving militia roles, tax records, the estimates of colonial governors or other interested and perhaps knowledgeable persons. None of this evidence is unbiased. Since it was collected for another purpose, it is subject to overt undercounting or overcounting depending upon the interests of the persons involved and the purposes for which it was collected. Certainly the available evidence from a variety of sources is not internally consistent. A casual check on the Massachusetts evidence available in Greene and Harrington,[5] for the period 1700 to 1720 lists two estimates for 1701 of 70,000 and 80,000 persons. In addition, figures for 1712 of 75,102, 1715 of 96,000, 1718 of 94,000 and 1721 of 94,000, reveal the wide variation between sources. Even the same sources often report widely inconsistent numbers. Governor Dudley for instance reported a population in 1709 of 56,000 and for 1715 of 75,102, an increase of 6 percent in six years with no evidence reported of a large immigration in any existing source. Clearly anyone who would like to construct estimates by decade of the population of the American colonies would be hard pressed in the face of such inconsistency to choose the most reliable evidence.

Nor does the problem stop there. It might be assumed that evidence which relied on actual counts such as militia roles, tax list, numbers of houses, etc., would be more reliable than the guesstimates of individuals. Such evidence, however, depends upon a reliable multiplier to expand the evidence to determine the total population. While both Greene and Harrington

TABLE III-1

Comparison of Sutherland and Rossiter Population Series

	Sutherland (Whites Only)			Rossiter (Whites Only)	
Year	Population	% Increase	Sutherland as a % of Rossiter	Population	% Increase
1620	102		1.03	99	
1630	4000	3821.6	1.82	2200	2122.2
1640	13,484	237.1	.77	17,605	700.2
1650	22,452	66.5	.83	26,820	52.3
1660	32,574	45.1	.90	36,238	35.1
1670	51,561	58.3	1.14	45,135	24.6
1680	67,992	31.9	1.12	60,530	34.1
1690	86,011	26.5	1.06	81,050	33.9
1700	91,083	5.9	.88	104,320	28.7

Growth Rate 1650 - 1700

Mean = 33.54
Standard Deviation = 17.68

Mean = 31.26
Standard Deviation = 4.17

Source: W. S. Rossiter, A Century of Population Growth from the First Census of the U.S. to the Twelfth 1790-1900, (Washington: GPO, 1909) and Historical Statistics of the United States, (Washington: GPO, 1960), p. 756.

and Sutherland explain the various multipliers,[6] it is clear that both sources feel these change between regions and over time, and that a range is perhaps most appropriate. The range of 1 to 4 to $5\frac{1}{2}$ suggested by Sutherland is clearly too wide for use in developing reliable population series. The upshot of the matter is that to determine the proper milita role multiplier, nothing short of the correct age-sex composition of the total population must be known. Such requirements have formerly exceeded the capacity of the available historical evidence. Hence, any estimate of total population by decade resulting from such evidence and methods must certainly be tentative since so much is left to the judgment of the investigator.

Let us now attempt to demonstrate the importance of the implicit hypothesis that Sutherland and Rossiter each held in their construction of the estimates for seventeenth-century colonial New England. Consider, for example, the role that immigration, emigration and catastrophe played in the selection of decade estimates by Sutherland. She implicitly must have assumed a steady flow of immigration through the port of Boston occurred up to the middle 1670's, when it was halted by the outbreak of King Phillip's War. Her decade growth rates of 66.5 percent in the 1640's, 45.1 percent in the 1650's, 58.3 percent in the 1660's, followed by a sharp decline thereafter (see Table 1) clearly reflect this hypothesis. Growth rates of this magnitude exceed substantially the maximum rates ever recorded by natural increase. Assumed immigration must have played an important part in her construction of population estimates.

It is difficult to analyze Rossiter's series in quite the same way. His estimates grow at approximately 31.3 percent per decade, a rate which indicates immigration or emigration remained constant. Since at the time Rossiter's estimates were made a concensus existed among historians that the natural rate of growth probably approached the Malthusian rate of 31 percent a decade, it is tempting to suppose that, despite his disclaimer, this view dominated his selection of estimates.[8] In either event, both Rossiter and Sutherland's estimates seem in part determined by their hypothesis about the course and causes of New England population growth. The use by scholars of either estimate, therefore, implicitly suggests the acceptance of the hypothesis underlying their construction.

Which of these two hypotheses appears most consistent with the historical evidence? Below we shall argue that there is little evidence for Sutherland's hypothesis and substantial support for the hypothesis we attributed to Rossiter. The great Puritan migration accounts for almost all of the immigrants into New England during the seventeenth century. Furthermore, except for the settlement of Long Island, these transplanted Englishmen and their offspring stayed in New England throughout the century. The nature of the initial immigration, the abundance of resources, and the absence of evidence of recurrent catastrophies suggests that population would have grown at a more or less regular rate. Our findings as to the average size of completed family (see Appendix B) also adds supporting evidence. The average size between decades fluctuated around an average of 7.13 children per family with a standard deviation of only .40. Thus the hypothesis we attribute to Rossiter appears the most reasonable. The important question to answer about the demographic history of colonial New England therefore becomes not whether fluctuations in the population's growth occurred, but what the actual rate of growth was.

The Stable Population Model

The direct measurement approach employed by both Sutherland and Rossiter cannot be used reliably to calculate either the rate of growth of the population or decade estimates. The necessary evidence simply does not exist. There is, however, a procedure that will allow the determination of the growth rate using indirect historical evidence that is sufficiently complete and reliable. The procedure termed the stable population model was developed some time ago by Alfred J. Lotka.[9] He has shown that under the conditions which are appropriate for a stable population, a knowledge of any two parameters will allow the estimation of the other parameters.

Lotka demonstrated that the value of the proportional rate of increase of a stable population is determined by the relation:

$$1 = \int_0^\infty e^{-ra} \mu(a) \; m(a) \; p(a) \; da$$

where $\mu(a)$ is the proportion of females married at age (a), m (a) is the maternity frequency among the married females and p(a) is the probability at birth of reaching age (a). Below we follow the methods and procedures suggested by Lotka to determine the natural rate of the population increase.

The stable population model implies that, given information about the proportion of married females in each age category, their maternal frequency and their life expectancy, we can derive a unique relationship between the average size of completed family and the natural rate of increase. While the evidence necessary to observe directly the seventeenth-century natural rate of increase does not exist, information is available on the average size of completed family (see Appendix B). Hence, the use of this model permits us to predict the natural rate of growth provided the conditions for stability are approximated.

The Assumptions of the Stable Population Analysis and the Conditions in Colonial New England

The stable population model is strictly applicable when migration into and out of a region is negligible, catastrophic mortality caused by epidemics and wars is absent, and systematic declines in fertility are lacking. While probably no area in historical time ever meets these criteria exactly, colonial New England closely approximated them between 1640 and 1700.

The great Puritan migration of the 1630's which populated New England with several closely knit families in the course of roughly one decade was unique to that region's colonial history. Between 1630 and 1643, somewhere around 18,500 to 21,500 Englishmen, women and children coming in family groups landed on the shores of New England, determined to carve a new civilization out of the wilderness.[10] Europeans had come before to fish and trade but only a handful attempted to stay permanently, the majority of which by 1630 were located in the Pilgrims' settlement at Plymouth. Probably the total of all Englishmen living in New England when the Puritans arrived was substantially fewer than 2000[11] and these persons were mostly men seeking quick fortunes by exploiting the resources of the area.

The Puritan migration lasted only a decade with immigrants ceasing to come in large numbers after 1643. Thereafter until the end of the French and Indian War at most only a few hundred came per decade and these were probably balanced by those returning.[12] Thus, before and after the 1630's few Europeans migrated to New England.

Following this large influx, native born New Englanders did not stay in areas in which they were born but generally migrated inland following the river valleys, founding new towns and settlements. Some in the 1720's migrated to the middle colonies and after 1763 thousands supposedly moved to the middle and southern colonies.[13] But generally New England between 1640 and 1700 seemed to approximate a closed society of pronounced British ancestry.

New England even more so than other New World areas appears to have been free of epidemics throughout the seventeenth century. There is little evidence, except for the diptheria epidemic of the last half of the 1730's that mass deaths ever occurred during the colonial period.[14]

Catastrophic mortality as a result of wars also appears to have been absent from the New England scene. Indian warfare throughout the latter half of the seventeenth century significantly affected the frontier settlement pattern. However, while many towns were destroyed or deserted, there is no indication that the population was seriously reduced. As the Indians rose in an attempt to reclaim their lands, most of the settlers avoided death by fleeing to the more populated, coastal areas.[15]

The results of our family sample (see in Appendix B) suggests no systematic decline or rise in fertility over the period.[16] New England women clearly were fertile from the beginning to the end of the seventeenth century. In general, colonial New England seems to closely approximate the conditions of a closed population necessary to apply a stable population model.

The Average Size of Completed Family and the Natural Rate of Increase

Given the above conditions we still require information about the female marriage and maternity structure and life expectancy. Fortunately, much of the recent research mentioned above has concentrated on developing this type of material. Utilizing these findings (see Appendix A) we can approximate both the marriage and maternal patterns and select a model or historical life table suited for our purposes. The relationship between the average size of completed family and the natural rate of increase of the population is given in Table III-2.

TABLE III-2

Predicted Relationship Between the Average Size of Completed Family and the Natural Rate of Increase

(1) r	(2) Married females	(3) Birth Rate/000	(4) Death Rate/000
.0000	3.43	23.9	23.9
.0050	3.94	27.7	22.7
.0100	4.54	32.2	22.5
.0150	5.21	36.9	21.9
.0200	5.99	41.8	21.8
.0225	6.42	44.4	21.5
.0250	6.85	46.9	21.9
.0264	7.13	48.4	22.0
.0275	7.35	49.6	22.1
.0300	7.85	52.2	22.2
.0325	8.38	54.9	22.4

The relevance of the assumptions that were employed in making these computations can be checked by comparing the predicted results of the model with the very complete demographic evidence from neighboring New France.[17] Colonists in New France for the generation running from 1700 to 1630 averaged (per completed family) 8.39 children. The birth rate for the same period averaged 55.8 per thousand and the rate of population increase, which for all practical purposes was the natural rate of increase, was .0318. Lotka's stable population model adapted for our purposes would associate an average size of completed family of 8.38 with an approximate natural rate of increase of .032 and a birth rate of 54.9. The difference between the predicted and observed natural rate of increase slightly more than two percent. The coincidence between the predictions and the model and the experience of French colonists in Canada is remarkably close.

Determining the Natural Rate of Increase

The determination of seventeenth-century New England's natural rate of increase now depends only upon estimates of the average size of completed family. It should be pointed out that the evidence on which this chapter is based constitutes a broader, more representative collection of quantative evidence than has previously been used in studies of the historical demography of colonial New England. Such studies as those of Graven, Lockridge, and Demos suffer from a serious restriction; they each deal with only one town. The advantage of these studies--greater detail and familiarity--is more than offset by the loss of a firm foundation for generalizations about the region. Our study of 1508 families, comprised of more than 10,000 persons, from twelve randomly selected Massachusetts towns reveals a great deal of cross sectional diversity (see Appendix B) in the average size of completed family. The particular characteristics such as the initial age and sex distribution of the founders, date of settlement, harvest failures, epidemics, Indian problems, etc., are the source of these diversities. Our approach overcomes this limitation by adopting a random sampling technique relying upon the law of large numbers. This law implies that the larger the random sample, the more confident the researcher can be that the characteristics of that sample are the same as those of the underlying population.

The primary sources from which the average size of completed family can be calculated or constructed are the New England Historical and Generalogical Register and the Vital Records of the Towns of Massachusetts to 1850. These lists, which include a large portion of the New England towns, are in general very carefully compiled from the registers of town clerks, church registers, county court records, cemetery inscriptions, and family records. This allows a fairly accurate compilation of the average size of completed family.

While our estimates do compare rather well with the findings of others, the study does contain possible limitations. For example, if no records existed for a town, it would automatically not be selected for study. Also, if there was general under-reporting of births, our average size of completed family may be too low. On the other hand, if small families were more apt to be excluded, our estimates may be too high. In any event, nothing can be done to ascertain the true direction and magnitude of these sources of bias. We can only point out their possible existence.

Our estimate of the average size of completed family as derived from the random sample are presented in Appendix B. In the absence of a trend we need only determine the average of the decade values to estimate the average size of completed family for the region. This average is 7.13 children (see Appendix B) and is associated in Table III-2 with a birth rate of 48.4 per thousand, a natural rate of increase of .0264 and an implicit death rate of approximately 22 per thousand. Thus, our predicted natural rate of increase for the New England populations is substantially lower than the Malthusian rate of .0313 which requires an average size of completed family of 8.13.

Let us now turn to a consideration of what can be said about the size of New England's population following what we have developed in previous sections of this chapter. By employing a stable population model and the average size of completed family we have determined the natural rate of increase of the New England population by decade. If we can establish the size of the existing population as of a certain date, say 1650, then by examining the evidence for immigration, it will be possible to estimate what the total population would be for succeeding decades.

It is, however, difficult, if not impossible, to establish definitely the population of New England before 1630. While prior to 1630 several thousand Englishmen lived along the shores of New England, the population was largely of a transitory nature, staying but long enough to make or break their fortunes. The few hundred persons who were there as of 1620 were mostly male. This number, by the 1630's, had grown by immigration to a few thousand, including the Pilgrims and the first of the Puritans. The great Puritan Migration, roughly 1629-1643, first established a white population in New England capable of reproducing itself. The number of Englishmen who transported themselves during this migration is uncertain, but a reasonable approximation can be made. The aggregate figure often recounted is that 65,000 during this time left England of which 18,000 to 21,200 went to New England.[18] A calculation on the basis of the tonnage of the ships involved allotting the customary ratio of one person per ton would result in between 23,400 to 25,032 English immigrants into New England. However, we know that higher than normal mortality plagued the early arrivals, that much equipment was brought by the Puritans and that some immigrants returned home in despair, thus making the one man one ton ratio appear too high.

It was after 1635, when the "starving time" was over, that the bulk of the Puritans came. The exodus to the Connecticut River also began about then, draining people out of Massachusetts. We know with some assurance that during 1637 Massachusetts attracted 1500 new arrivals and in 1638 over 3000 more as the migration continued.[19] The pace slackened during 1639 and was definitely over by 1643. It appears from our examination that the population of Massachusetts was approximately 12,500 in 1640.[20] Sutherland estimates 8,932 persons and Rossiter, 14,000.

These Puritans seem to have come as families and we know that the families who began having children in the 1640's immediately after arrival had an average 1.15 fewer children than families who began their fertility in the 1650's (see Appendix A). This reflects the fact that often children born in England and coming as immigrants were not entered in the lists from which our family reconstruction was made. Judging from the 1640 average size of completed family, 6.95, we would expect the initial growth rate to be lower. However, in light of the bias mentioned above, it seems reasonable to assume that the early immigrants experienced approximately the same rate of natural increase established for later generations. Assuming that the population of Massachusetts was 12,500 in 1640, that 1,000 more came in 1641, then the population due to natural increase (.0264) per year would probably have been about 17,000 by 1650.

Outside the estimated 17,000 persons residing in Massachusetts in 1650, were a number of people residing in areas that became known as Maine, Rhode Island, Connecticut, New Hampshire, Long Island and also Plymouth, which was later absorbed by Massachusetts. Both Rossiter and Sutherland are in essential agreement as to the total population in these places in both 1630 and 1640. What fragmentary evidence that was available seems to substantiate their estimates as reasonable but it should be acknowledged that these are clearly educated guesses. Sutherland and Rossiter's estimates, which begin to diverge substantially after 1640, are 20 percent apart by the start of the sixth decade. The major area of disagreement between the two series is over the population of Connecticut. Sutherland thinks almost 2,000 fewer persons were located there than does Rossiter. Since there is no reliable basis to choose between the two estimates, we have selected the average of the two or 9,780 people living in New England outside of Massachusetts in 1650. Hence, our base population for New England in 1650 is about 27,000. This is approximately the same as the Rossiter estimate but is about 16 percent higher than Sutherland's.

The establishment of a base population in 1650 along with our previously determined natural rate of population growth allows us to calculate population purely as a result of natural increase by decade from 1650 to 1700. Assuming no net migration into or out of New England, our results are shown in Table III. It should be noted that our estimate for 1700 is almost exactly between those of Sutherland and Rossiter.

TABLE III-3

Total New England Population by Decade (1650-1700)

r = 1.2978/decade	
1650	26,780
1660	34,755
1670	45,105
1680	58,537
1690	75,970
1770	98,594

Independent Test of Results

It is highly desirable to have an independent check upon our results -- a test using information not used in developing our estimates. This is a procedure neither Sutherland nor Rossiter could employ. The most complete actual numeration that would allow us to check our estimate is the militia role for 1690. The respective governors of the colonies of New England were required to submit a compilation based upon an actual count of the number of men trained for military service in 1690. All did and their reports to the Board of Trade have survived. The reporting is very detailed, generally being given by towns. The militia list for the five New England political areas totals 15,288, which must be enlarged somewhat to include New Englanders on Long Island. This number times the appropriate multiplier gives us an independent check upon the total population. The difficulty with this procedure as previously indicated is to determine the correct multiplier.

The multiplier chosen for converting militia to total population is of crucial importance. Generally estimates range about 5, although some go as low as 4 and as high as 6. Such a range obviously produces population estimates with large variances. Since the multipliers given by Felt (5-1/3), Dexter (4-1/2 to 5-1/2),[21] and those suggested by various governors have little empirical basis, we have attempted to construct a more meaningful figure. Determination of the percentage of population within age groups will facilitate this calculation.

Fortunately, implicit in our estimates of the vital statistics is a corresponding age distribution of the population. As a result, it is possible to obtain the percentage of the population that was male and over 16 years of age. This figure deflated for exemptions allows the calculation of the appropriate multiplier for the militia role. We will take as a parameter the rate of natural increase of 2.642 percent per year. The first task in deriving the age structure is the determination of life expectancy in New England and then the selection of the appropriate United Nations model life table consistent with our findings. While the 1838-54 English life table closely followed the historical evidence for New England females (see Appendix A), it did not in the case of males. Seventeenth-century New England males clearly lived longer than their eighteenth-century counterparts in the mother country. For seventeenth-century Andover, Mass., Greven, for example, suggests that the average age at death of males and females reaching age 21 was 64.2 and 61.6 respectively.[22] The English life table for males predicts that life expectancy at age 21 was 59.8, a substantial difference. To be consistent for both males and females it was necessary to select another life table, one that more clearly corresponds to New England's historical experience. The United Nations model life tables which were developed precisely for such purposes were employed.[23] The $^{o}e_{20}$ (life expectancy at age 20) for various levels in the United Nations model life table are shown below in Table III-4. Assuming there is little difference between $^{o}e_{20}$ and $^{o}e_{21}$, it appears that Greven's observed expectations correspond to level 65 for males and level 45 for females, which have $^{o}e_{o}$'s (life expectancy at birth) of 52.5 and 42.5, respectively. Implicit in Greven's findings is that seventeenth-century New England males could expect when born to live 12.6 years longer than males born in England two centuries later. Females, however, had about the same life expectancy as English females two centuries later. The perils of childbirth remained the main stumbling block to a long life.

By expanding the $_{n}L_{x}$ values (the survivors within an age group) as shown in Table III-5, we can construct the stable population age structure. The resulting age distribution of the population when stability is attained is presented in Table III-6. Results indicate that those in what was known as the alarm class, comprised of all males between 16 and 60, account for approximately 28 percent of New England's seventeenth-century population. Adult males 16 and upward or polls make up 31 percent of the total inhabitants. The deficiency between the alarm establishment and polls is 0.1 or about one ninth as J. B. Felt suggested.[24]

TABLE III-4

Comparison of Life Expectancy at Age 20 Under Various Assumptions

	Males			
^oe_o	50	52.5	55	57.6
level	60	65	70	75
To	4872	5117	5357	5613
T_{20}	3281	3486	3687	3898
l_{20}	75.9	78.3	80.6	83.1
$^oe_{20}=\frac{T_{20}}{l_{20}}+20$	63.23	64.5	65.8	66.9
	Females			
^oe_o	42.5	45	47.5	50
Level	45	50	55	60
To	4344	4606	4866	5131
T_{20}	2842	3060	3280	3502
l_{20}	70	73	75	78
$^oe_{20}=\frac{T_{20}}{l_{29}}+20$	60.6	61.9	63.73	64.89

Note: $^oe_{20}$ using the English life table 1838-54 is 60.29 and is very close to that for level 45 (women).

$^o3_{21}$ using the English life table is 60.63 which compared with Greven's estimate of 61.6.

Source: Values for the various levels of life expectancy were taken from "Methods for Population Projection by Sex and Age," United Nations Population Studies, #25, 1956.

TABLE III-5

Computation of the Age Distribution of the Population

	Level 65 Males					Level 45 Females		
Age	${}_nL_x$	$r(x + \frac{n}{2})$	$e^{-r(x+\frac{n}{2})}$	1.027 ${}_nL_x e^{-r(x+\frac{n}{2})}$	%	${}_nL_x$	${}_nL_x e^{-r(x+\frac{n}{2})}$	%
0–4	42,783	.0661	.9361	41,131	16.6	40,675	38,076	17.9
5–9	40,720	.1982	.8202	34,300	13.7	37,456	30,721	14.5
10–14	40,135	.3302	.7047	29,047	11.7	36,491	25,715	12.1
15–19	39,526	.4624	.6298	25,566	10.3	35,521	22,371	10.5
20–24	38,623	.5944	.5519	21,892	8.8	34,208	18,879	8.9
25–59	37,561	.7266	.4836	18,655	7.5	32,686	15,807	7.4
30–34	36,480	.8586	.4238	15,878	6.4	31,116	13,187	6.2
35–39	35,355	.9908	.3713	13,482	5.4	29,528	10,964	5.2
40–44	34,022	1.1228	.3254	11,370	4.6	27,899	9,078	4.3
45–49	32,398	1.2549	.2851	9,486	3.8	26,140	7,453	3.5
50–54	30,320	1.3871	.2498	7,778	3.1	24,124	6,026	2.8
55–59	27,654	1.5191	.2189	6,217	2.5	21,740	4,759	2.2
60–64	24,244	1.6513	.1918	4,776	1.9	18,816	3,609	1.7
65–69	19,985	1.7833	.1681	3,450	1.4	15,249	2,563	1.2
70–74	14,962	1.9155	.1473	2,263	.9	11,130	1,639	.8
75–79	9,679	2.0475	.1290	1,282	.5	6,897	890	.4
80–84	5,027	2.1796	.1130	583	.2	3,357	379	.2
85 plus	2,249	2.3118	.0991	229	.09	1,734	172	.08
				247,385			212,288	

TABLE III-6

Age-Sex Distribution of the Population

Age	Males as a % of total	Females as a % of total
0-4	8.95	8.28
5-9	7.46	6.68
10-14	6.32	5.59
15-19	5.56	4.87
20-24	4.76	4.11
25-29	4.06	3.44
30-34	3.45	2.87
35-39	2.93	2.38
40-44	2.47	1.97
45-49	2.06	1.62
50-54	1.69	1.31
55-59	1.35	1.04
60-64	1.04	.78
65-69	.75	.56
70-74	.49	.36
75-79	.28	.19
80-84	.13	.08
85 plus	.05	.04
	53.80	46.17 = 100

Knowing that 28 percent of the population is male between 16 and 60, the remaining task is to determine what percentage of this class is included on the militia lists. Douglass remarked in 1742 that "the alarm list males from age 16 and upwards, is about one third more than the training list, because many are excused from impresses and quarterly trainings."[25] This estimate is in sharp contrast with the 13 percent deficiency between able bodied men and militia in Barbadoes in 1684.[26] Since the first appears to be little more than a rough approximation and the second is for an area with very different characteristics, it was necessary to derive further estimates for New England. Relying upon militia roles and censuses which exist for New York around the turn of the seventeenth century, it is possible to determine militia as a percentage of population. In years where the militia lists and censuses do not coincide, we have allowed the lagging number to grow at a yearly rate of .02642 for the appropriate number of years. The results listed in Table III-7 show that on average men on the militia lists are 75.8 percent of the alarm class.

TABLE III-7

Estimate of Militia as a Percentage of Alarm Class

Year	Militia	Men (Polls) x .90=Alarm Class (Men 16-60)	Males 16-60	Militia as % of Alarm Class
1693	2932			
1698	3340	4559		73.3
1700	3182			
1703	3441		4487	76.7
1721	6000			
1723	6321	8175		77.3
				75.8 (Average)

Source: Greens and Harrington, American Population before the Federal Census of 1790, pp. 92-96.

Utilizing the above information, it is possible to develop a more accurate multiplier. Given 31 percent of the population are males 16 and above, 90 percent of these adult males are polls 16-60, and 75.8 percent are militia members, we would estimate that 21 percent of the total population is in the militia. In other words, the number of militia to all inhabitants was one to 4.72. Applying this multiplier to the militia role by colony and for New England yields the estimates for total population given in Table III-8. The total population of New England in 1690 figured on this basis is 75,721 persons as compared to our estimate of 75,970 shown in Table III-3. The small difference of approximately one percent certainly lends support to our estimate.

Estimation of 17th Century Labor Force

Having established a time series for the number of New England inhabitants and their age-sex distribution, we can now turn to the final step in our analysis of population. For any economy in which land is relatively abundant and capital relatively unimportant in the production function, accurate measurement of the labor force is crucial to our understanding of the path of economic growth. Since the scope of the labor supply will vary according to economic and social conditions and the age-sex distribution of the inhabitants, we must examine each during the seventeenth century. In the event that these conditions remain unchanged, we would expect the labor force as a percentage of total population to also remain constant. This appears to have been the case throughout the latter half of the seventeenth century in the northern colonies.

TABLE III-8

1690 Population as Estimated via the Multiplier Approach

	Mass.	Conn.	Plymouth	R.I.	N.H.	English in New York*	Total
Militia	9,292	3,058	1392	792	754	755	16,043
Total Population	43,858	14,434	6570	3738	3559	3562	75,721

Multiplier = 4.72

*In calculating the total population of New England on the basis of militia, it is important that we include inhabitants who migrated outside the political confines of New England. During the seventeenth century the English struggled long and hard with the Dutch for their share of New York. In the process English colonists from New England established themselves on eastern Long Island in what was to become the county of Suffolk and in the county of Westchester. Hence, we have included in the 1690 militia list an estimate of English fighting men in New York. By taking the 1693 estimate of 816 militia and decreasing it by our yearly growth rate (.02642), we estimate that in 1690 there were 755 militia in Suffolk and Westchester counties.

Source: Greene and Harrington, American Population Before the Federal Census of 1790.

By 1650 New England had established herself as a competitor in the commercial sector. In addition she was mining her valuable natural resources and producing agricultural commodities for both home consumption and export. Since all of these industries continued throughout the rest of the century and no important new industries started, it is reasonable to conclude that demand factors had little affect on the proportion of the total population gainfully employed.

Attitudes toward woman and child labor also continued unchanged for the last half of the century. Despite legislation such as an act passed in 1656 aimed at forcing "woemen, girles, and boyes" into the textile industry,[27] women and children maintained their traditional roles in the home and on the farm. The lack of evidence suggesting social changes which would alter employment patterns implies that the labor force over the century remained a definite proportion of persons in each sex-age category.

Finally the stability of the age-sex distribution of the inhabitants is an implicit result of the demographic model applied above. Given constant fertility, unchanged life expectancy, and an isolated population (i.e., negligible migration or catastrophic mortality), the New England population would tend toward a stable age-sex distribution for the period in question.

The question that remains is what proportion of the total population was gainfully employed. Unfortunately, the surviving souces do not provide the necessary information to compute this percentage directly. Hence, we must rely upon qualitative descriptions of the Puritan economy to help calculate the labor force. For our purposes we follow closely the definition of labor force used by Stanley Lebergott in his study of <u>Manpower in Economic Growth</u>: "it consists of those persons in the labor market at any given time."[28]

We include only those occupations outside the home, hence eliminating a very large portion of potential women and child workers.

Let us first consider the female segment of the labor supply. At an early age the girls undertook such household chores as cooking, sewing, washing, cleaning and even some farm chores from which we obtain the term "milkmaid." Undoubtedly some girls were sent out at an early age to become servants but "there was little likelihood of their ever following any career but that of a housewife."[29] We should not, however, conclude that no women were in the labor force. The society did have some widows and spinsters who were seeking work outside the home. Alice Hanson Jones estimates for 1774 that "about 10 percent of the women aged 21 and over would have been widows."[30] We assume that this percentage approximates the number of adult females included in the seventeenth-century labor supply.

For males the percentage gainfully employed was considerably higher than that of females. Younger boys also put in much time helping around the home, but by the age of ten to fourteen a boy usually chose his calling. At this point he was sent out for training through a seven year apprenticeship. Therefore, we will assume that on average, males entered the labor force at age 12. He probably continued working at his chosen occupation throughout his able-bodied years which, on the basis of the alarm class measure, ended at approximately age 60.

Combining all males between 12 and 60 and 10 percent of the adult females, we find that approximately 36.3 percent of the total population was gainfully employed. Alternatively, by using Lebergott's male percentage for 1880 (87.2 percent of males ten and over) and female percentage for 1830

(7 percent of all white females), we find that 35.8 percent were in the labor force.[31] Since there is little reason to expect a substantial change between 1800 and the latter half of the seventeenth century, we have concluded that 36 percent of the inhabitants made up the labor supply. The results in Table III-9, coupled with the above assumptions, show that the labor force was growing at a rate of about 2-1/2 percent per year. To the extent that land and capital remained relatively abundant during the seventeenth century thus minimizing the effects of diminishing returns to labor, the above results give a lower-bound estimate of the growth of aggregate output. Hence, it would appear that New England's pace of extensive growth between 1650 and 1700 was high by most standards.

TABLE III-9

New England
Labor Force by Decade

(1650 - 1700)

1650	9,641
1660	12,512
1670	16,238
1680	21,073
1690	27,349
1700	35,494

Labor Income

To complete the calculation of labor income, we must combine the above determined quantities of labor with their appropriate wage rates. But first the appropriate wage rates must be established. Since the dearth of all colonial price series including wages renders direct calculation impossible, it is necessary that we use the most reliable alternative. Recalling the theoretical model in Chapter II, it was concluded that through the commercial sector New England wages were equated with those in the mother country, thus making English wages a good proxy. By examining the seventeenth-century English wage rates, it will be possible to establish at least the trend of labor payments in New England.

Although better than the New World data, English sources for the seventeenth century are not as numerous or as accurate as one might like. For the purposes of this discussion, I shall concentrate on two main sources: first I will examine English seamen's wages as presented by Ralph Davis in The Rise of the English Shipping Industry, Chapter VII; alternatively, I will develop average wages from the various occupations listed in James E. Thorold Rogers' A History of Agricultural Prices in England, 1583-1702, Vol. V. Let us examine each in turn.

By studying the wage records of the High Court of Admiralty, Davis has compiled a time series of seamen's wages between 1604 and 1775.[32] The portion of this series relevant to this study is shown in Table III-10. While the general trend in seventeenth-century English seamen's wages is upward, the large fluctuations due to wars should be noted. During an era when ocean conflict dominated English warfare, we would expect a rise in the remuneration of crewmen to compensate them for the added risk of war. This risk payment is the amount over and above the average wage necessary to attract labor in to English shipping. Therefore, since our interest here is in obtaining a

TABLE III-10

ENGLISH SEAMENS' WAGES, 1630-1720

Year	Wage s/ month	War Years
1630-1651	19.5	
1652-1654	34.0	x
1655	23.5	
1656-1660	34.0	x
1661-1664	20.0	
1665-1667	36.5	x
1668-1671	28.5	
1672-1674	37.5	x
1675-1677	27.5	
1678	30.0	x
1679-1688	24.5	
1689	45.0	x
1690-1694	55	x
1695-1696	45	x
1697-1702	24.5	
1708-1711	47.5	x
1712-1717	24.5	
1718	30.0	x
1719-1720	24.5	

Source: Ralph Davis, The Rise of the English Shipping Industry, pp. 135-37.

proxy for the average New England wage whether on land or sea, it is desirable to isolate the risk payment included in the above series. To accomplish this task, I have regressed the Davis series on time using the dummy variable technique to separate information on risk:

$$\text{English Seamen's Wage} = 18.0496 + 0.113119 \cdot (\text{time}) + 17.3225(D) + e$$

$R^2 = 0.80085$ (5.8932) (16.1251)

$\bar{R}^2 = 0.79605$

Noting that the influence of war years was statistically significant, I have estimated the decennial averages of New England wages on the basis of the constant term and the coefficient for time both of which are also significant at the 99% level. The results of this prediction are shown in Table III-11.

As an alternative series I have taken a simple average of the wages for carpenters, masons, laborers to artisans, and for digging, hedging or ditching.[33] These classes are assumed to be representative of the average wage of English craftsmen and were chosen because each listed the wage rate per laborer in shillings per day and because each was relatively complete. In order to compare this series with that of seamen, the daily wage rates are converted to monthly on the assumption that craftsmen worked six days per week. The resulting decennial averages shown in Table III-11 indicate that English craftsmen received higher nominal wages than did seamen. This discrepancy might well be explained by the fact that, in addition to their nominal wages, seamen also received provisions while on board. When the cost of this victualling which is placed near 16 shillings per month for the seventeenth century[34] is added to the nominal wage, the differential is greatly reduced, moreover the similarity in the wage rates suggests that indeed the English labor market was competitive.

During the course of the seventeenth century, seamen's and craftsmen's wages rose at approximately the same rate until the tenth decade when craftmen's wages show a marked increase. The trend in the seamen's series is certainly consistent with Douglass C. North's conclusion "......that from the mid-seventeenth century onward productivity (in shipping) rose at a significant rate. . . ."[35] Combining these figures with the rapidly growing labor force predicted in Table III-9, produces my estimates of average payments to labor by decade shown in Table III-11 and Chart III-1. The series based upon the remuneration to vessel crewmen indicates that labor's share of regional income was growing at a rate of about 34% per decade or 3% per year. Alternatively, craftmen's wages show that during the 1690's nominal labor payments began to grow at an annual rate of 4 rather than 3 percent. In an area where labor was such an important factor of production, it seems unlikely that changes in payments to the other factors or changes in the aggregate price level would offset this impressive rate of growth. Hence, on the basis of the return to labor, it appears that seventeenth-century New England was experiencing both extensive and intensive economic growth.

TABLE III-11

PAYMENTS TO LABOR
1650-1709

	Labor Force[a] (1)	Nominal Seamens' Wage[b] s/month (2)	Nominal Seamens' Wage plus victualage Ł/year (3)	Wage Bill(Ł) col. 1 x col. 3 Ł/year (4)	Nominal Craftsmens' Wage[c] Ł/year (5)	Wage Bill(Ł) col. 1 x col. 5 Ł/year (6)
1650-59	11,076	22.19	22.16	242,896	19.33	214,131
1660-69	14,375	22.84	22.84	328,268	20.15	289,714
1670-79	18,655	23.52	23.52	438,777	20.89	389,751
1680-89	24,211	24.20	24.20	585,856	21.83	528,623
1690-99	31,412	24.89	24.89	782,207	24.95	783,904
1700-09	40,779	25.55	25.55	1,042,067	27.46	1,119,873

Sources:

[a]Table III-9.

[b]Davis, The Rise of English Shipping Industry, pp. 135-37.

[c]Roger, A History of Agricultural Prices in England, Vol. V, pp. 664-670.

CHART III-1

AGGREGATE PAYMENTS TO LABOR BASED UPON
ALTERNATIVE WAGE SERIES
1650-1709
£(000)

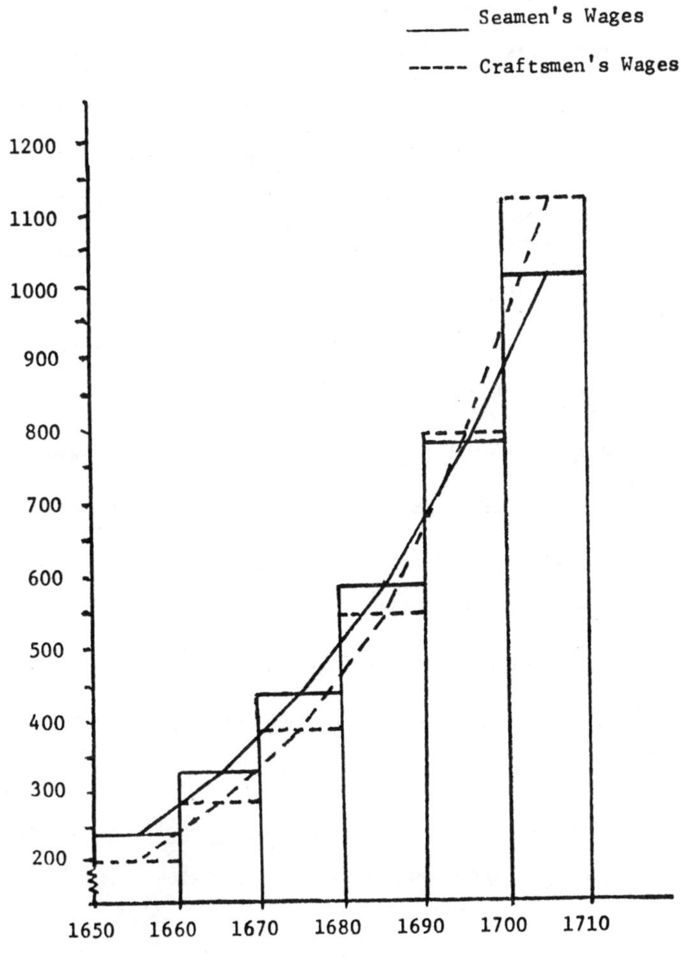

FOOTNOTES FOR CHAPTER III

1. For the most recent books dealing with the demographic issue, see Philip J. Greven, Four Generations: Population, Land and Family in Colonial Andover, Massachusetts (Ithaca: Cornel University Press, 1970); John Demos, A Little Commonwealth, family Life in Plymouth Colony (New York: Oxford University press, 1970); Kenneth A. Lockridge, A New England Town--The First Hundred Years: Dedham, Massachusetts 1636-1736 (New York: W. W. Norton & Company, Inc., 1970). Also see Maris A. Vinovakis, "The 1789 Life Table of Enward Wigglesworth," JEH, XXXI, (Sept. 1971), pp. 570-590;Danial Scott Simth, "The Demographic History of Colonial New England," JEH, XXXII (March 1972), pp. 165-183; and Maris A. Vinovakis, "Mortality Rates and Trends in Massachusetts Before 1860," JEH, XXXII (March 1972), pp. 184-213.

2. W. S. Rossiter, A Century of Population Growth from the First Census of the United States to the Twelfth 1790-1900, (Washington: GPO, 1909).

3. Franklin B. Dexter, "Estimates of Population in the American Colonies," American Antiquarian Society, Oct. 1887, pp. 22-50.

4. Stella H. Sutherland, "Estimated Population of American Colonies: 1610-1780," Historical Statistics of the United States (Washington, D.C.: GPO, 1960), p. 756.

5. Evarts B. Greene and Virginia D. Harrington, American Population Before the Federal Census of 1790 (Gloucester, Mass.: Peter Smith, 1966), p. 14-15.

6. Historical Statistics, p. 743 and Greene & Harrington, p. xxiii.

7. For a discussion of the Malthusian growth rate, see T. R. Malthus, An

Essay on the Principle of Population, 1798 as reprinted in the Royal Economics Society Reprint of 1926, pp. 20-21. Also see "The Growth of Population in America, 1700-1860," by J. Potter published in Population in History, edited by D. V. Glass and D. E. C. Eversley.

8. Rossiter, A Century of Population Growth, p. 10.

9. For the original development of this model, see Alfred J. Lotka, Elements of Physical Biology (Baltimore: Williams & Wilkins Co., 1925). The application of this model by the author to colonial population is found in "The Size of American Families in the Eighteenth Century," American Statistical Association, 1925.

10. Bernard Bailyn, The New England Merchants, p. 16.

11. Greene & Harrington, American Population, p. 8.

12. A review of the colonial population literature reveals the lack of direct quantitative estimates of immigration. Qualitatively, however, there is little indication of substantial immigration to New England following the Puritan movement. Also, while there is some record of families returning to England or moving to other parts of the New World to seek their fortunes, out migration appears negligible. This is not surprising when one considers the tight family structure that social historians have adequately described. Hostility toward strangers was enough to turn most newcomers away especially when compared to the friendly propsects in Chesapeake region. For a discussion of the lack of migration to New England after the Great Migration, see James H. Cassedy, Demography in Early America (Cambridge, Mass.: Harvard University Press, 1969), pp. 40 & 175.

13. Cassady, *Demography in Early America*, pp. 40 & 233.

14. Robert Higgs and H. Louis Stettler, III, "Colonial New England Demography: A Sampling Approach," *William and Mary Quarterly*, Third Series, XXVIII, (April 1970), pp. 282-294.

15. For a discussion of the influence of Indian warfare, see Lois Kimball Mathews, *The Expansion of New England* (New York: Russell & Russell Inc., 1962), pp. 443-75.

16. The following linear regression with average size of completed family as the dependent variable and time as the independent variable shows the slope co-efficient to be insignificant at any level.

$$AFS = 7.44 - 0.124\ \text{Time} + e$$

$$(-1.192) \qquad r^2 = 0.424$$

17. Jacques Hearipin, *La Population Canadienne Au Debut Du XVIII Siecle Nuptialite-Mortalite Infantile* (Presses Universitaires De Frances, 1954), pp. 39 & 50.

18. Charles Edward Banks, *The Planters of the Commonwealth, 1620-1640* (Boston: Houghton Mifflin, 1930), p. 12.

19. Darrett B. Rutman, *Winthrop's Boston*, p. 179.

20. For complete estimates of the growth of Massachusetts population between 1630 and 1650, see Rutman, *Winthrop's Boston*, p. 179.

21. Joseph B. Felt, "Statistics of Towns in Massachusetts," Collections of the *American Statistical Association*, Vol. I, part II, pp. 136-38.

22. Greven, *Four Generations*, pp. 193 and 196.

23. "Methods for Population Projection by Sex and Age," published in the United Nations Population Studies #23, 1956.

24. Felt, "Statistics of Towns," p. 137.

25. William Douglass, A Summary, Historical and Political, of the First Planting, Progressive Improvements, and the Present State of the British Settlements in North-America (London: R. & J. Dodsley, MDCCLX), Vol. I, p. 531.

26. William & Mary Quarterly, Third Series, Vol. 26, #1, p. 7.

27. Bailyn, New England Merchants, p. 75.

28. Stanley Lebergott, Manpower in Economic Growth (New York: McGraw Hill Book Co., 1964), p. 30.

29. Edmond S. Morgan, The Puritan Family (New York: Harper & Row, 1944), p. 67.

30. Alice Hanson Jones, "Middle Colonies," p. 112.

31. Stanley Lebergott, "Labor Force and Employment, 1800-1960," Output, Employment and Productivity in the U.S. after 1800, in Studies in Income & Wealth, Vol. 30 (Princeton, N.J.: Princeton University Press, 1966), p. 134, and Manpower in Economic Growth, p. 519.

32. Ralph Davis, The Rise of the English Shipping Industry, pp. 135-37.

33. James E. Thorold Rogers, A History of Agricultural Prices in England (Oxford: Clarendon Press, 1887), Vol. V, pp. 664-670.

34. Davis, The Rise of Shipping, p. 145.

35. North, "Sources of Productivity Change," p. 954.

CHAPTER IV

WEALTH AND ITS COMPOSITION

In any study of income, regional or national, our primary concern is with how the flow of production arises. In the previous chapter we concentrated upon labor's role in the New England economy and concluded that indeed it was an important one. But this is by no means the entire story, for it is man combining his energies with natural and man-made resources that produces the final output. Hence to complete the measurement of regional income in seventeenth-century New England, we must examine the payments to land and capital.[1]

To compute land and capital's share in the productive process, I have conducted a detailed study of individual wealth holdings. Below I will present a new time series of New England wealth estimates which were obtained from a random sample of the surviving estate inventories.[2] Though these estimates are not the primary goal of this study, they do give some idea of the economic endowments available to the New England colonists and do provide a base with which to compare wealth data for later periods. It should, however, be noted that these figures are at best a very rough approximation of economic well being for they make no account of human resources (excepting slaves or servants) and do include items which contribute little to the productive process.

The primary goal of this investigation was to discern the composition of asset holdings in order to establish the stock of productive land and capital held by the society. After deciding exactly which assets to include as land and capital, the stock values were taken directly from the probate records. These stock figures are presented below and will be converted into decennial income payments in the final chapter.

The data in this chapter will be presented in two distinct classes. Following the discussion of asset categories will be estimates of decedent wealth patterns drawn from the sample of inventories. However, since the sample is only representative of deceased wealth holders, caution must be exercised when making inferences about land and capital holdings of the living. The final portion of the chapter will therefore be devoted to the link between the assets of the living and dead. By making the necessary age correction, it will be possible to estimate per capita holdings of wealth and productive assets for the living.

Classification of Probate Data

To ensure equity in the distribution of estates, the New England forefathers had laws which required that the executor and at least two honest persons should "make and draw up a true and perfect inventory of all his (the testator's) goods, chattells, wares, merchandize, as well moveable as not moveable, and one draught thereof he (the executor) shall deliver up to the head officer of the towne."[3] Many of these early estate inventories have survived to provide economic historians with one of the few sources of measurable data for the colonial period. While some of the records are incredibly detailed, others are frustratingly incomplete with items grouped without respect to homogeneity. Some studies of the probates have focused upon detailed price and quantity data to determine market trends for various commodity groups such as consumer and producer durables, inventories, financial assets, etc. to establish the composition of individual wealth holdings.[4]

But the goal here is to develop series on the value of productive factors categorized as land and capital. Let us examine each category.

Obtaining land values from the probate inventories involved a straight forward summation of the recorded values. In keeping with the colonial New England tradition of accurately recording transactions involving land, estate recorders methodically listed all real estate. Included in these listings were land, buildings, and improvements whose values in most cases could not be separated. The house, barn, out buildings, and home lot were often listed in one unit, but real estate was never found mixed with other commodities. It was difficult to determine the quantity of land for the appraiser most often used imprecise measures as parcels, pieces, and fields rather than acres. Real estate such as warehouses, docks, piers, and saw mills was kept separate from the other land holdings making it possible to consider these items as capital used in the commercial or resource sectors. In conclusion land values contained herein are comprised mainly of acreage, including fences, bridges, roads, etc., housing and all farm buildings.

The measurement of capital holdings proved more difficult, for this productive factor is less well-defined. The decision to include only those commodities relating most directly to market production was based upon modern-day national income accounting. To obtain a clearer understanding of the problem, the reader is referred to the inventories shown in Plate IV-1 and in Appendix C. From these illustrations it is immediately apparent that in colonial New England's frontier economy, market related capital is not easily distinguishable. For example, weaving equipment may have been used entirely for household production or may have been part of an artisan's

PLATE IV-1

Inuentory Joseph Pomiry

An Inventory of the Estate of Joseph Pomry Estate taken after his wifes desea[s] taken october 1674 41

Imprimis:

a hous and 15 acers of Land or thar about	60-00-00
to a tabell and to Joynt Stools	00-15-00
to a bed 3 pillows & 1 rugg	04-07-06
to 2 pare of blenckets	01-02-00
to his best waring Clos on Jacket & briches and hat	01-15-00
to on bedsted & a cheest	00-13-00
to on Iron poot pothuks tramell a wetter bucket a barell & a gun	01-04-06
to 2 basket on yard of broadcloth	00-13-06
to 2 old porengers on old platter one old Chaphin poot	00-04-06
to woden war and tenen pan	00-03-00
to on Childs Chare and Small books	00-42-06
to on Hefer which was sold for	04-10-00
to a frien pan	00-03-00
to a par of Cards	00-01-03
to a Spining whell	04-04-00
to a Small bottell	00-01-06
to a Sow and 3 pigs	00-15-00
to 2 old hatts	00-04-00
to a siue	00-00-09
to the womans waring Clos	00-15-00
	77-15-00

this inventary was taken by us and aprised as witnes our hand.

John Barsham
Wm his [mark] Cotton marke

Browne to have his 12 out of the moueables as it is fined
Elias Stileman Clerk

producer capital; leather and cloth may have been consumer goods or part of a business inventory; and agricultural equipment such as churns, firkins, funnels, etc. may have been either consumer or producer durables. Hence, the classification of capital was somewhat arbitrary depending largely upon the occupation of individual decedents.

After thoroughly studying the inventories it was decided that capital values would be collected in three separate categories, working capital, fixed capital and shipping capital.[5] While for the regional income estimates this breakdown is unnecessary, it was hoped that this detailed information would provide insight into the distribution of capital payments between the important shipping sector (see Chapter II, pp. 34-7) and other endeavors. The value of capital within each group was collected per probate inventory following these general guidelines:

A. Working Capital -- Items included in this class were all those likely to be sold in the market: livestock (all types); farm inventories of crops such as wheat, corn, peas, hay, etc., but not consumer goods such as butter, cheese, honey, etc.; inventories of fish, timber, and furs; wool and hides; business inventories of finished goods usually found in stores. Cash was also included in this category.

B. Fixed Capital -- These are durable items used for further market production in sectors other than shipping: vehicles such as carts, wagons, and canoes; farm implements comprising plows, harrows, harnesses, saddles, etc.; saw mills and grist mills; fishing equipment including boats, nets, and hooks; tools of the artisan as well as those of the farmer (hammer, saws, axes, wedges, hetchels, hoes, shovels, sickles, hooks, bettle rings, etc.);

trapping equipment; scales and steelyeards; containers such as barrels, hogsheads, bags, troughs, pails and the like; lumber, iron, and nails. This category most often did not include weapons, kitchen utensils such as pots, pans, grid irons, or churns, or weaving implements (looms, wheels, shuttles, spindles, wool cards, etc.).

C. Shipping Capital -- This class comprises all investments related directly to the New England shipping industry: ocean-going vessels such as ketches, shallops, sloops, and ships; warehouses; docks and piers; compasses, sails and other rigging.

Decedent Wealth Patterns

Shown in Table IV-1 are the decade averages of decedent wealth by county.[6] The gross wealth listed here is composed of all estate property both real and personal. The sum for each individual was usually listed in the inventory, but care in gathering the figures was necessary since additions were sometimes incorrect.[7]

Data in Table IV-1 is presented by political areas so that we might better understand differences within the New England economy. With one exception all areas show a distinct upward trend in average decedent wealth during the latter half of the seventeenth century. Of those experiencing increases Essex County between the seventh and eighth decades enjoys the highest percentage rise; the passage and enforcement of the Navigation Acts which stimulated all shipping within the British empire may have strongly affected wealth holdings in this commercially oriented county. The exception to the rising trend was New Hampshire where the exact opposite pattern is noted. In this northern-most colony average decedent wealth was declining

TABLE IV-1

AVERAGE[a] INVENTORY WEALTH PER DECADE, 1650-1709
(in £ per head)

	Essex		Bristol		New Haven		Fairfield	
	Percent of inventories > £ 200	Average Wealth	Percent of inventories > £ 200	Average Wealth	Percent of inventories > £ 200	Average Wealth	Percent of inventories > £ 200	Average Wealth
1650-59	42.00	185.86						
1660-69	35.00	190.48			31.00	223.15		
1670-79	35.00	283.49			34.00	222.91	46.00	240.31
1680-89					49.00	258.61	49.00	252.41
1690-99			51.00	254.68	54.00	318.87	50.00	308.46
1700-09			45.00	230.66	50.00	316.77	53.00	273.35

	Hartford[b]		New Hampshire		New England[c]	
	Percent of inventories > £ 200	Average Wealth	Percent of inventories > £ 200	Average Wealth	Percent of inventories > £ 200	Average Wealth
1650-59	40.00	249.61			42.00	217.73
1660-69	46.00	325.86	45.00	286.31	35.00	254.45
1670-79	44.00	288.57	33.00	268.45	36.00	260.75
1680-89	48.00	331.81	30.00	285.12	47.00	281.98
1690-99	53.00	335.26	37.00	234.35	51.00	290.32
1700-09	48.00	241.01	22.00	179.82	47.00	282.07

[a]County averages are obtained by taking a weighted average of estates totaling greater than £ 200 and less than £ 200. See Appendix

[b]The first three decades for Hartford County are estimated from inventory abstracts, see footnote

[c]Average New England wealth is a simple average of each county.

in all but the decade of the 80's. Again we cannot rule out sampling error, but a relative contraction of the resource sector including fish and furs might well have been responsible for the falling average wealth. It should also be noted that in nearly all cases the first decade of the eighteenth century saw a decline in average wealth. Nonetheless, the six decades following New England's entry into the Atlantic commercial world on average show an increase in wealth holdings.

For those who feel that these average figures paint "too rosy a picture of the standard of living,"[8] a rising trend in the median also suggests improvement. During the era there is a general increase in the percentage of decedents with wealth greater than ₺200. In fact, for the last thirty years of the study nearly half of the estates fall into this category.

When compared with colonial estimates circa 1774, the seventeenth-century inventory data implies that the New England colonies sustained their economic growth during the following century. If we extend mean wealth for 1700-1709 at the average decennial rate for the previous 60 year period (5.6%), we predict 1770-1779 wealth to be 413.05. This compares quite well with the Jones figure of ₺472.50.[9]

Turning to the composition of wealth, the pattern of land holdings follows very closely that of the aggregate estate. (See Table IV-2). Again all areas except New Hampshire exhibit a rising trend in land holdings over the last five decades of the seventeenth century and a decline for the ensuing decade. Moreover, as shown in Table IV-3, during the 60 years between 1650 and 1709 the overall tendency was for an increasing proportion of the total estate to be held in land. In terms of the model presented in Chapter III

TABLE IV-2

AVERAGE INVENTORY LAND AND CAPITAL HOLDINGS
(in £ per head)

	Essex		Bristol		New Haven		Fairfield	
	Land	Capital	Land	Capital	Land	Capital	Land	Capital
1650-59	59.64	94.79						
1660-69	95.48	59.96			55.94	110.74		
1670-79	167.65	91.28			59.30	97.21	126.07	67.60
1680-89					163.24	55.82	153.43	59.02
1690-99			148.90	66.74	183.41	72.88	194.59	63.02
1700-09			144.77	51.68	179.54	70.80	170.70	53.68

	Hartford		New Hampshire		New England	
	Land[a]	Capital[b]	Land	Capital	Land	Capital
1650-59	151.17	55.73			105.40	75.26
1660-69	200.08	74.57	124.16	125.81	118.91	92.77
1670-79	176.47	65.08	128.86	95.66	131.67	83.37
1680-89	208.93	71.99	99.91	87.15	156.37	68.49
1690-99	199.84	85.05	108.30	64.27	167.00	70.39
1700-09	161.06	42.92	116.09	33.10	154.43	50.44

[a]Estimate of land holdings for the first 3 decades are based upon the following regression equations estimated from the data from 1680-1709:

1) $L_{£\,200^-} = -15.52 + \underset{(13.7934)}{0.63}\,W + e \qquad R^2 = .7066$

2) $L_{£\,200^+} = 13.08 + \underset{(30.2117)}{0.62}\,W + e \qquad R^2 = .89245$

[b]Capital was estimated from the following equation also obtained from 1680-1709 data:

1) $K = 2.80 + \underset{(7.4445)}{0.23}\,W + e \qquad R^2 = .41229$ 2) $K = -28.46 + \underset{(12.9253)}{0.27}\,W + e \qquad R^2 = .60298$

TABLE IV-3

PERCENTAGE DISTRIBUTION OF LAND, CAPITAL, AND OTHER ASSETS, 1650-1709

	Essex			Bristol			New Haven			Fairfield		
	Land	Capital	Other	Land	Capital	Other	Land	Capital	Other	Land	Capital	Other
1650-59	32	51	17									
1660-69	50	31	19				25	50	25			
1670-79	59	32	9				27	44	29	54	28	18
1680-89							63	23	14	61	23	16
1690-99				58	26	16	58	23	19	63	20	17
1700-09				63	22	15	57	22	21	62	20	18

	Hartford			New Hampshire			New England		
	Land	Capital	Other	Land	Capital	Other	Land	Capital	Other
1650-59	61	23	16				48	35	17
1660-69	61	23	16	43	44	13	46	38	19
1670-79	61	23	16	48	36	16	50	32	18
1680-89	63	22	15	35	31	34	55	24	21
1690-99	60	25	15	46	27	27	57	24	19
1700-09	67	18	15	65	18	17	55	18	27

we can interpret this pattern as an absolute expansion of the agricultural sector with increasing rents to land. However, we cannot be entirely sure of whether or not the overall rise in land holdings was due to an increase in the size of farms or a rise in the relative price of land. In comparing the real estate portion of wealth with later periods, we find that land and structures in seventeenth-century inventories was a smaller percentage, approximately 50 percent in seventeenth-century New England, and 63 percent in later eighteenth-century Middle Colonies.[10] This result is hardly surprising when one considers increased scarcity of land and the improved quality of housing between the two periods.

Turning to portable assets used in market production we encounter a trend exactly opposite that of real estate (see Table IV-2). With the exception of the slight rise in the 1660's the absolute level of capital holding declined throughout the period in question. It should, however, be pointed out that the lack of data for the more urban, commercial counties during the latter half of the period may indeed introduce a downward bias into the capital estimates. To the extent that these areas were engaged in enterprises which relied upon labor and capital for their output, we would expect decedents to hold relatively more of their estates in portable productive assets. The percentage of New England estates held in capital also exhibits a distinct decline over the period while the average percentage between 1650 and 1709 is more than twice that of a later date, 32 percent for the seventeenth century compared to 18 percent for circa 1774.[11] From these figures it would appear that capital was decreasing in its relative importance.

A further breakdown of the data on productive assets into categories of working, fixed, and shipping capital in Table IV-4 reveals less distinct trends but does provide insight into productive processes. Essex County,

TABLE IV-4

PERCENTAGE DISTRIBUTION OF WORKING, FIXED, AND SHIPPING CAPITAL, 1650-1709

	Essex			Bristol			New Haven			Fairfield		
	Working	Fixed	Shipping	Working	Fixed	Shipping	Working	Fixed	Shipping	Working	Fixed	Shipping
1650-59	90	6	4									
1660-69	84	12	5				91	8	1			
1670-79	85	7	8				94	5	1	90	10	0
1680-89							85	15	0	86	14	0
1690-99				86	14	0	79	15	5	90	10	0
1700-09				83	14	3	84	10	6	86	14	0

	Hartford			New Hampshire			New England		
	Working	Fixed	Shipping	Working	Fixed	Shipping	Working	Fixed	Shipping
1650-59							90	6	4
1660-69				89	11	0	88	10	2
1670-79				66	28	6	84	13	3
1680-89	88	12	0	59	15	6	80	14	6
1690-99	88	12	0	62	12	26	81	13	6
1700-09	81	18	1	57	31	12	78	17	5

the urban and commercial representative in the sample, does experience a slight increase in shipping capital, an observation consistent with the expansion of the commercial sector. Also noteworthy is the expansion of New Haven's shipping capital during the late seventeenth and early eighteenth centuries. This certainly lends support to Rutman's contention that the New England market was intimately connected by the water of Long Island Sound.[12] While the New Hampshire figures show wide variations, the relatively heavy concentration of fixed and shipping capital is best explained by existence of fishing vessels, drying racks, nets, saw mills, etc. associated with the resource sector. The high percentage of working capital in the rural counties is due to the large holdings of livestock and foodstuff inventories.

Before turning to the calculation of wealth of the living population, a final disintegration of the sample data is revealing. By classifying the decedents according to occupation we can examine relationships between economic endeavors and wealth. Since most probates did not list the decedent's occupation it was necessary to infer this from commodities in the inventory. For example, persons owning ships or portions thereof, docks, warehouses, etc., were classified as merchants. Persons with large acreage, livestock, foodstuffs, plows, etc. are considered farmers while those holding small fishing vessels, nets, traps, saw mills, etc. are thought to be employed in the natural resource sector. Artisans, laborers, sailors, and those for whom an occupation was not discernable are included in the category of "others." By far the largest portion of the decedent population was engaged in tilling the soil, with the group including artisans, laborers, and sailors running second and merchants and "resource men" vying for third and fourth. It would appear as though there is a slight increase in farm employment and a decrease in commercial and other employment over the six decades. This conclusion, however, is somewhat tenuous in light of the fact that for the last three decades when this trend is most notable we have no estimates for Essex County. Excluding such urban centers would undoubtedly bias employment statistics since we would expect these areas to have the highest concentration of laborers, artisans, sailors, and merchants and the smallest concentration of farmers. Nonetheless, we can compare these statistics with Professor Jones' findings for 1774.[13] Not surprisingly, averages for the earlier period indicate that a higher proportion of the decedents were farmers, 65% compared with 54% for 1774; fewer were merchants, 3% compared with 14% for 1774; and only slightly fewer were "others," 27% compared with 32% for 1774.[14]

Inventory totals in Table IV-5 reveal that merchants were clearly the most wealthy both in terms of the mean and the median estate. By the very nature of their occupation they held the most total capital and certainly the highest percentage of shipping capital. On the basis of average wealth between 1650 and 1709, farmers, on the other hand, ranked third with the majority of their estates being held in land. Individuals employed in the resource sector ranked second though decennial averages were subject to wide variation. As might be expected, the category including laborers and sailors possessed the smallest amounts of physical wealth. Undoubtedly these persons were mostly endowed with human capital, an asset not included in the probate inventories.

TABLE IV-5

ASSET HOLDINGS BY OCCUPATION, 1650-1709
(in £ per head)

	Percentage with wealth > £ 200	Percentage within each occupation per decade	Percentage within each occupation per decade excluding Essex Co.	Wealth	Land	Working Capital	Fixed Capital	Shipping Capital
Farmers								
1650-59	45	58		183.89	67.99	82.99	5.33	.41
1660-69	61	63	74	292.59	134.86	98.71	8.11	.41
1670-79	69	57	57	396.69	259.69	82.84	8.68	.35
1680-89	67	75	75	383.07	244.78	73.42	9.97	
1690-99	65	70	70	378.62	248.34	63.54	9.46	
1700-09	65	70	70	351.66	237.09	58.07	8.45	
Merchants								
1650-59	100	04		350.80	45.88	203.50	2.92	73.00
1660-69	67	03	3	647.50	151.66	337.78	3.00	82.25
1670-79	83	06	9	1,022.82	282.80	498.56	21.93	106.83
1680-89	100	01	1	665.70	33.33	279.60	76.25	126.67
1690-99	100	01	1	781.19	171.80	359.56	6.27	130.00
1700-09	100	02	2	413.82	102.00	149.82	13.02	31.60
Resources								
1650-59		00						
1660-69	20	05	9	171.38	88.24	34.63	26.70	
1670-79	42	03	4	507.29	203.85	157.95	104.98	
1680-89	50	03	3	400.99	284.30	35.09	34.02	
1690-99	81	04	4	509.67	227.47	93.51	58.16	28.28
1700-09	67	03	3	254.40	141.81	32.88	27.75	13.91
Other								
1650-59	20	36		146.31	40.25	64.07	5.64	
1660-69	17	29	14	106.86	38.77	27.87	10.94	
1670-79	3	32	30	80.31	31.74	38.13	1.28	
1680-89	13	19	19	95.62	47.25	13.05	3.56	
1690-99	29	22	22	156.27	60.05	54.38	5.57	
1700-09	25	23	23	117.99	48.87	24.97	6.01	

<u>Wealth Estimates for the Living Population</u>

The extensive literature utilizing estate records to estimate per capita wealth repeatedly emphasizes the need for age correction when inferring wealth of the living from that of the dead, and this study is no exception.[15] The sample from the probate inventories will be a biased representation of the living population for two reasons: 1) the age distribution of probated individuals compared to that of the living will contain more older persons; and 2) a positive correlation exists between age and aggregate wealth. To correct for this bias Alice Hanson Jones attempted to place decedents in her sample into one of three age groups. After calculating the mean decedent wealth per age group, she assumed that living persons within each age class held equivalent wealth and restructured "the inventory data, using the age distribution of the living for relative proportions rather than that of the dying probates."[16] However, as any student of genealogy can verify, the task of such age classification is a formidable one and often produces indefinite results. To avoid this costly process I have hence devised an alternative method of age correction.

This method requires knowledge of three parameters which are then used to estimate average wealth per age group, A_i: 1) total wealth of the sample for a given time period, W_t; 2) number of decedents within each age group, n_i; and 3) percentage distribution of wealth by age, k_i. Total wealth of the probate population, W_t, is available from the information in Table IV-1 and Appendix D. By multiplying the weighted average wealth per area by the number of sampled decedents we can establish the total wealth of the sample.

Given a sufficient amount of information on the ages of wealth holders, we could restructure the inventory data in terms of age groups. The total could then be expressed as a function of the number of individuals within each age class and the average wealth per class:

$$W_t = \sum_{i=1}^{m} n_i \cdot A_i$$

where n_i is the number of decedents within age group i and A_i is the average wealth for that group. In the absence of the necessary age data we can estimate n_i on the basis of the stable population used in Chapter III. Recalling the discussion of life expectancy,[17] it was established that the $^o e_o$'s (expectation of live at birth in years) for seventeenth-century New England males and females were 52.5 and 42.5, respectively. On this basis we can enter the United Nations Model Life Table III, Survivors to Exact Age[18] and compute the percentage of the population dying within each age class. To establish a base population it is necessary to assume that only persons reaching age 20 are potential wealth holders. By dividing this figure, 78,304 for males and 69,900 for females, into the number of decedents ages 20-25, 26-44, and 45 and older we obtain the results shown in Table IV-6. These percentages times the number of probates sampled in each political area yield estimates for n_i.

The remaining task in calculating values for the average wealth per age class, A_i, is the specification of the percentage distribution of wealth by age. To accomplish this in the absence of sufficient age data, I have assumed that $A_i \ldots\ldots A_{m-1}$ can be expressed as constant percentages, $k_{1 \ldots m-1}$, of A_m. Under this assumption total wealth for the three age groups, 20-25,

26-44, and 45 plus, can be expressed as follows:

$$W_t = n_1 \cdot A_1 + n_2 \cdot A_2 + n_3 \cdot A_3 \tag{1}$$

where $$A_1 = k_1 \cdot A_3 \tag{2}$$

$$A_2 = k_2 \cdot A_3 \tag{3}$$

Hence, $$W_t = n_1 \cdot k_1 \cdot A_3 + n_2 \cdot k_2 \cdot A_3 + n_3 \cdot A_3 \tag{4}$$

$$= A_3(n_1k_1 + n_2k_2 + n_3) \tag{5}$$

and $$A_3 = W_t/(n_1k_1 + n_2k_2 + n_3) \tag{6}$$

Values for the constant percentages were chosen from the New England data circa 1770[19] on the assumption that the percentage distribution of wealth with respect to age changes little over time. To test the reliability of this assumption I have run a pilot study of Hartford County for the years 1650 to 1680 using the abstracts of estate inventories.[20] Though exact ages were not available for any decedents, many of the abstracts did contain a list of the individual's children and their wages from which I inferred the parent's age. Assuming that persons married in their early twenties and began raising families after the first two years, I placed decedents with children ranging in age from 2 to 18 in the age class of 26 to 44 and decendents with children over 18 or with grandchildren in the age class of 45 and older. Persons with no children, young wives left to the care of a parent, or estates willed to their parents were classified between the ages of 20 and 25. From this pilot study it was found that average inventories in the youngest group were 21 per cent of average inventories in the oldest group while those in the middle group were 59 percent. These findings compare with later estimates of 14 and 57 percent respectively and thus lend support to the assumption of a constant percentage distribution over time.[21] However, since the Jones data is based upon a more detailed genealogical study, I will consider her estimates to be more reliable.

The values of average wealth, land and capital holdings by age group presented in Tables IV-6 and 7 provide the basis for computing average wealth of the living. The data on land and capital holdings by age class is computed according to the procedure described above for aggregate wealth except that the percentage distribution, k_i, for land and capital is different. Again following Alice Hanson Jones I have assumed that persons aged 20 through 25 held approximately one-tenth the land and one-fifth the capital of older people, while persons aged 26 through 44 held one-half the land and seven-tenths the capital.

Knowing the distribution of wealth by age allows us to now infer the asset holdings of the living population. For a certain portion of the living within each age bracket it is assumed that their wealth is similar to that in the probate sample. However, in light of the relatively small number of surviving inventories, it is clear that many decedents were not probated and hence that the sample is not representative of a large segment of the living population. For example, in his study of the seventeenth-century Essex County, Davisson suggests that the surviving inventories represent only about twenty-five percent of the original records.[22] For the present work, this percentage is adopted as representative of seventeenth-century New England as a whole.[23]

TABLE IV-6

AVERAGE WEALTH BY AGE CLASS, 1650-1709
(in £ per head)

WEALTH

	Essex			Bristol			New Haven			Fairfield		
	A_1[a]	A_2[b]	A_3[c]	A_1	A_2	A_3	A_1	A_2	A_3	A_1	A_2	A_3
1650-59	28.37	115.53	202.68									
1660-69	29.08	118.40	207.72				34.10	138.71	243.35			
1670-79	43.28	176.21	309.15				34.03	138.56	243.09	36.69	149.37	262.06
1680-89							39.48	160.75	282.02	38.54	156.90	275.26
1690-99				38.88	158.31	277.73	48.68	198.21	347.73	47.09	191.74	336.38
1700-09				35.21	143.38	251.54	48.36	196.90	245.44	41.73	169.91	298.09

	Hartford			New Hampshire			New England		
	A_1	A_2	A_3	A_1	A_2	A_3	A_1	A_2	A_3
1650-59	38.11	155.15	272.20				33.24	135.34	237.44
1660-69	49.75	202.55	355.35	43.71	177.96	312.22	39.15	159.41	279.66
1670-79	44.06	179.38	314.70	40.98	166.87	292.75	39.81	162.08	284.35
1680-89	50.66	206.25	361.84	43.53	177.23	310.93	43.05	175.27	307.50
1690-99	51.18	208.40	365.61	35.78	145.67	255.56	44.32	180.46	316.60
1700-09	36.79	149.81	262.82	27.45	111.78	196.10	43.06	175.33	307.60

A_1 = ages 20-25

A_2 = ages 26-44

A_3 = ages 45+

[a] $A_1 = k_1 \cdot A_3 = 0.14 \cdot A_3$

[b] $A_2 = k_2 \cdot A_3 = 0.57 \cdot A_3$

[c] $A_3 = W_t / (n_1k_1 + n_2k_2 + n_3)$

where W_t = weighted average of wealth (w_t) · number of inventories (N),

$k_1 = 0.14$,

$k_2 = 0.57$,

and n_1, n_2, n_3 = number dying in A_1, A_2, A_3

= % dying in A_1, A_2, A_3 · number of inventories (N).

Therefore $A_3 = w_t \cdot N/N(0.0341 \cdot 0.14 + 0.1221 \cdot 0.57 + 0.8437)$

$= w_t/0.9179)$

TABLE IV-7

LAND AND CAPITAL HOLDINGS BY AGE CLASS, 1650-1709
(in £ per head)

LAND

	Essex			Bristol			New Haven			Fairfield		
	A_1[a]	A_2[b]	A_3[c]	A_1	A_2	A_3	A_1	A_2	A_3	A_1	A_2	A_3
1650-59	9.11	33.39	65.47									
1660-69	11.53	53 45	104.81				6.75	31.32	61.51			
1670-79	20.24	93.85	184.03				7.16	33.20	65.09	15.22	70.58	138.39
1680-89							19.71	91.39	179.19	18.53	85.89	168.42
1690-99				17.98	83.36	163.45	22.15	102.68	201.33	23.50		213.60
1700-09				17.48	81.05	158.91	21.68	100.51	197.08	20.66	9 5.56	187.38

	Hartford			New Hampshire			New England		
	A_1	A_2	A_3	A_1	A_2	A_3	A_1	A_2	A_3
1650-59	18.25	84.63	165.94				12.73	59.01	115.70
1660-69	24.16	112.01	209.63	14.99	69.51	136.29	14.36	66.57	130.53
1670-79	21.31	98.79	193.71	1 5.56	72.14	141.45	15.90	73.71	144.53
1680-89	25.23	116.96	229.34	12.06	55.93	109.67	18.88	87.54	171.65
1690-99	24.13	111.87	219.36	13.08	60.63	118.88	20.17	93.49	183.32
1700-09	19.45	90.17	176.79	14.02	64.99	127.43	18.65	86.45	169.52

A_1 = ages 20-25

A_2 = ages 26-44

A_3 = ages 45+

TABLE IV-7 (continued)

CAPITAL

	Essex A_1[d]	Essex A_2[e]	Essex A_3[f]	Bristol A_1	Bristol A_2	Bristol A_3	New Haven A_1	New Haven A_2	New Haven A_3	Fairfield A_1	Fairfield A_2	Fairfield A_3
1650-59	22.23	70.74	101.05									
1660-69	14.06	44.75	63.92				25.97	82.64	118.06			
1670-79	21.41	68.12	97.31				22.80	72.54	103.64	15.86	50.45	72.07
1680-89							13.09	41.66	59.51	13.84	44.04	62.92
1690-99				15.65	49.81	71.15	17.09	54.38	77.69	14.78	47.03	67.19
1700-09				12.12	38.51	55.10	16.61	52.84	75.48	12.59	40.06	57.22

	Hartford A_1	Hartford A_2	Hartford A_3	New Hampshire A_1	New Hampshire A_2	New Hampshire A_3	New England A_1	New England A_2	New England A_3
1650-59	13.08	41.59	59.41				17.65	56.16	80.23
1660-69	17.50	55.65	79.50	29.51	93.89	134.1	21.76	69.23	98.90
1670-79	15.26	48.56	69.38	22.44	71.39	101.98	19.55	62.21	88.88
1680-89	16.88	53.72	76.75	20.44	65.04	92.91	16.06	51.11	73.02
1690-99	19.95	63.47	90.67	15.07	47.96	68.52	16.51	52.53	75.04
1700-09	10.07	32.03	45.76	7.76	24.07	35.29	11.83	37.64	53.77

[a]Land holdings for $A_1 = k_1L_3 = .11\ L_3$

[b]Land holdings for $A_2 = k_2L_3 = .51\ L_3$

[c]See Table IV-6, footnote a. $L_t = L_3\ (.911)$

[d]Capital holding for $A_1 = k_1K_3 = .22\ K_3$

[e]Capital holding for $A_2 = k_2K_3 = .20\ K_3$

[f]See Table IV-6, footnote a. $K_t = K_3\ (.938)$

For the probate-type living wealth holders the step from the sample data shown in Tables IV-6 and 7 to the estimates of living wealth shown in Table IV-8 is a simple matter of weighting the former by the age distribution of the potential wealth holding population. Referring to Table III-6 these weights are computed by summing the number of wealth-holding males and females. It is assumed that 100 percent of all males 20 and older are potential wealth holders. Moreover, it is estimated that the percentage of potential wealth holders among females aged 20-25, 26-44, and 45 plus is 11%, 12% and 13% respectively.[24] Weights for the three age brackets are .22, .47 and .31, respectively, and are substantially different from those for the decedent population. As a result of this distribution, the average assets of the probate-type living wealth holder is much lower than that of the probated individual.

Estimates of the assets of the nonprobate-type living are necessarily much less reliable since we have no record of their estates. We can only infer the differences between these and the inventories sampled by asking why certain probates were not registered with the courts. A portion of the difference between the number of surviving inventories and the number of dying wealth holders can undoubtedly be explained by the fact that probates have either been lost or destroyed. For these cases there is no reason to believe that on average estate values were different from those in the sample. On the other hand many of the nonprobated individuals must have left little or no wealth, left no debts, or distributed their estates prior to death. Since under these circumstances we might expect estate wealth to be much less than that probated, I will assume that nonprobate-type estate values were about one-half the probate-type.[25]

By weighting probate and nonprobate-type wealth appropriately, it is possible to arrive at the final estimates of the average wealth, land, and capital per living wealth holder.[26] These series when multiplied by the total number of living wealth holders provide estimates of the wealth which will be used in the following chapter. It should be noted, however, that the stock of both land and capital increase until the final decade when the capital stocks decline absolutely.

Finally, before moving on to regional estimates, let us compare New England's wealth with that of the mother country. For the purposes of comparison, I shall use average wealth per head shown in the last column of Table IV-8. Although I know of no English wealth figures for this early date, it is possible to obtain a rough estimate from Gregory King's figures on yearly income.[27] By multiplying his average income figure for 1688, ₤7.9, by an upper-bound wealth multiplier of five,[23] we find that wealth per head in the mother country was roughly ₤39.5. Though the accuracy of this figure leaves much to be desired, it can be compared with my 1680-89 estimate,Correcting for the difference in exchange rates,[29] seventeenth-century New England wealth was ₤32.77, suggesting that during the latter half of that century average wealth between the two regions was approximately the same. By this comparison it would appear that the seventeenth-century New England colonists had attained a relatively high standard of living.

TABLE IV-8

WEALTH, LAND, AND CAPITAL HOLDINGS OF THE LIVING, 1650-1709

Decade	Population	Potential Wealth Holders[a] 20-25	26-44	45+	Total	Average Probate type	Ave. per[b] nonprobate-type	Ave. per living[c] wealth holder	Ave. per head
					WEALTH (£)				
1650-59	30,767	1,876	4,091	2,651	778,464	144.52	72.26	90.33	25.30
1660-69	39,930	2,435	5,309	3,441	1,189,972	170.22	85.11	106.39	29.80
1670-79	51,821	3,160	6,890	4,466	1,570,196	173.08	86.54	108.17	30.30
1680-89	67,253	4,101	8,942	5,795	2,203,669	187.16	93.58	116.98	32.77
1690-99	87,282	5,322	11,605	7,521	2,944,517	192.69	96.35	120.44	33.74
1700-09	113,275	6,908	15,061	9,761	3,712,727	187.22	93.61	117.01	32.78
					LAND (£)				
1650-59					354,631	65.84	32.92	41.15	11.53
1660-69					519,208	74.27	37.14	46.42	13.00
1670-79					717,236	82.24	41.12	49.41	13.84
1680-89					1,150,060	97.67	48.84	61.05	17.10
1690-99					1,594,010	104.31	52.16	65.20	18.26
1700-09					1,912,684	96.45	48.23	60.28	16.89
					CAPITAL (£)				
1650-59					295,770	54.91	27.46	34.32	9.61
1660-69					473,237	67.69	33.85	42.31	11.85
1670-79					551,898	60.83	30.42	38.02	10.65
1680-89					658,953	49.97	29.99	34.98	9.80
1690-99					784,781	51.36	25.68	32.10	8.99
1700-09					729,790	36.80	18.40	23.00	6.44

Footnotes to Table IV-8

[a]To compute the wealth of the living it was first necessary to estimate the age distribution of the potential wealth holders from the stable population model. In doing so it was assumed that all males over 20 were potential wealth holders. The sample of inventories shows that 91.2% of the surviving records belonged to males while 8.8% belonged to females. These percentages are assumed to hold for the entire wealth holding decedent population. From this information it is possible to solve for the percentage of females that were potential wealth holders within age groups. Let X equal the potential number of probates, M_i and F_i equal the percentage of males and females in age group i, N equal the total population, F^p equal the females in age group i, F_i^t equal the total population of females in age group i, and F_i^p/F_i^t equal the percentage of potential female wealth holders. Assuming all males over 20 are potential wealth holders, it follows that:

1) $$0.912X = \sum_{i=1}^{n} M_i \cdot N$$

2) $$0.088X = \sum_{i=1}^{n} F_i^p$$

3) $$\sum_{i=1}^{n} F_i^p = \frac{0.088}{0.912} \left(\sum_{i=1}^{n} M_i \cdot N\right)$$

4) $$\sum_{i=1}^{n} F_i^t = \sum_{i=1}^{n} F_i \cdot N$$

5) $$\frac{\sum_{i=1}^{n} F_i^p}{F_i^t} = \frac{0.088}{0.912} \left(\sum_{i=1}^{n} \frac{M_i}{F_i}\right.$$

Hence the percentages of potential female wealth holders within each age group are 11%, 12%, and 13% respectively.

[b]Average wealth for the nonprobate type wealth holder equals 50% of Average Probate type.

[c]Average wealth per living wealth holder equals 25% of Average Probate type plus 75% of Average Nonprobate type.

FOOTNOTES FOR CHAPTER IV

1. It is recognized that natural resources such as fish and furs were also production inputs. But since these resources were held in common, the returns to them were completely dissipated by entrants into the resource sector, i.e., $p_{nr} = p_r \cdot MPP^{r}_{nr}$ which implies that natural resources are utilized until the value of their marginal physical product is equal to their zero price.

2. For a complete discussion of the sampling technique used for this survey, see Appendix C.

3. Records of the Colony of Rhode Island, vol. I, p. 188.

4. See Jones, "Middle Colonies" and "New England Colonies."

5. For an alternative classification of capital, see Jones, "Middle Colonies," pp. 36-42.

6. The estimates in this chapter are nominal in that they have not been corrected for changes in the price level.

7. I am grateful to Professor Davisson, University of Notre Dame, for pointing out in our correspondence that aggregate value figures in the Essex County inventories were quite inaccurate.

8. Jackson Turner Main, "Comments on Papers by Jones, Shepherd and Walton, and McCusker," JEH, XXXII (March 1972), p. 158.

9. This figure was computed by adding total physical wealth and financial assets including cash for all ages. See Jones, "New England Colonies," p. 114.

10. _Ibid._, p. 107.

11. The figure for 1774 is obtained by summing Jones' estimates of indentured servants and slaves, producer durables, producer perishables, business inventories, and cash. _Ibid._, p. 108.

12. Rutman, "Governor Winthrop's Garden Crop," pp. 407-409.

13. Jones, "New England Colonies," p. 126.

14. Findings such as these are extremely useful if we hope to establish the importance of the sectors relative to one another and make statements about shifts over time. Further research on Essex and Suffolk Counties would most certainly increase the reliability of the estimates.

15. Jones, "Middle Colonies," pp. 7-8 and "New England Colonies," pp. 113-14; Lampman, Chapter II; Mendershausen, "The Pattern of Estate Tax Wealth."

16. Jones, "New England Colonies," p. 14.

17. See Chapter III, p. 62.

18. _UN Population Studies_ #25, pp. 76-77.

19. Jones, "New England Colonies," p. 114.

20. _A Digest of the Early Connecticut Probate Records_, Vol. I, compiled by Charles William Manwaring.

21. Total wealth for these figures was computed by summing "total physical wealth" and "financial assets, including cash" for each age group. Jones, "New England Colonies," p. 114.

22. Davisson, "Essex County Price Trends: Money and Markets in 17th Century Massachusetts," _Essex Institute Historical Collection_, CII (April 1967), p. 150.

23. For the eighteenth century Alice Hanson Jones finds that 33% of the estates were inventoried. Hence the 25% estimate may in fact represent a lower bound.

24. For a discussion of this estimation see Table IV-10.

25. Alice Hanson Jones followed a similar assumption in her study of New England. She feels that this is high in light of her estimate of 29% for the Middle Colonies. Jones, "New England Colonies," pp. 116-17.

26. See Table IV-8.

27. G. N. Clark, The Wealth of England from 1496 to 1790 (London: Oxford University Press, 1946), pp. 192-93 and Sidney Pollard and David W. Crossley, The Wealth of Britain (London: B. T. Batsford, Ltd., 1968), p. 153.

28. Jones, "Middle Colonies," p. 129.

29. Chever, "Commerce of Salem," p. 125.

CHAPTER V

NEW ENGLAND'S REGIONAL INCOME FROM 1650-1709

The discussion in the previous chapters of the New England economy and its factors of production paves the way for the final measurement of seventeenth-century regional income. The remaining task is to combine the factor payments to labor, land, and capital. Labor's share has already been calculated and requires no further manipulation. Land and capital, on the other hand, have only been discussed in terms of their stock values and must be converted to yearly flow values if they are to have meaning in an income sense. Once these conversions have been carried out, the estimation of regional income is straight forward. The resulting series will be compared with qualitative evidence for the era and with estimates for later dates.

Income Estimates

As the first step in the estimation of aggregate factor payments, we examined the work force and the payments to labor. By assuming that equilibrium wage rates in New England were at least equal to those in the mother country and multiplying these rates times the average labor force per decade, we concluded that labor's share of regional income (in nominal terms) was growing at a compound rate of approximately 3 percent per year. Deflating labor's share by the consumer price index we constructed (see Appendix E), we find that real labor payments rose over ten fold between 1650 and 1709 or at a yearly rate of about four percent. In light of the rapid population growth during the period, such extensive growth is hardly startling and has long been recognized by economic historians.[1] Factoring out this population growth, real labor payments per head rise at a rate of 1-1/2 percent per annum indicating a distinct improvement in labor's productivity.

The yearly returns to land and capital can be added to the labor payments to arrive at a final estimate for New England's extensive and intensive growth. However, yearly rental series, like most other data for this early period, do not exist, thus making it necessary to compute them from the stock values of land and capital developed in Chapter IV. Assuming that all assets earned at least a normal rate of return, we can convert these stocks to flows by discounting by the market rate of interest. Rates for the northern colonies are few and scattered, but the general trend during the seventeenth century appears to have been downward. New England courts, for example, adopted a maximum legal rate of 8 percent which was lowered in 1693 to 6 percent,[2] a pattern not unlike that occurring at the same time in England. In fact, under the assumption that the supply of capital to New England was perfectly elastic at the English price,[3] it is appropriate to discount the stock values by the English rates.[4] During the century in question, the English legal rate on commercial loans fell from 10 percent to 6 percent with the latter prevailing from 1651 to 1714.[5] Using this legal rate as a reasonable proxy for the market discount rate, I have estimated yearly payments to land and capital in Table V-1. It is realized that the use of a single interest rate for the entire sixty-year period will not reflect short-term fluctuations in the capital market. However, since this study is primarily interested in secular trends, the use of an appropriate single rate in the absence of large changes over the long run is not a serious defect. Furthermore, as can be seen in column 7 of Table V-1, discounting by several rates within a conceivable range makes little difference in the resulting final rates of growth. The remainder of this discussion will, therefore, be couched in terms of the 6 percent rate.

TABLE V-1

REGIONAL INCOME ESTIMATES UNDER 3 DISCOUNT RATES[(a)]
1650-1709

	1	2	3	4	5	6	7
	Wage Bill[(b)] Ƀ/year	r = .06 Land Payments[(c)] Ƀ/year	Capital Payments[(d)] Ƀ/year	Aggregate Income = 1+2+3	Money Income per head	Real Income per head	Percentage Change in col.6
1650-59	228,513	21,278	17,746	267,537	8.70	4.89	
60-69	308,991	31,152	28,394	368,537	9.23	5.49	12
70-79	414,264	43,034	33,114	490,412	9.46	8.92	62
80-89	557,239	69,004	39,537	665,780	9.90	9.90	11
90-99	783,055	95,641	47,087	925,783	10.61	12.34	25
1700-09	1,080,970	114,761	43,787	1,239,518	10.94	13.67	11
		r = .08					
1650-59		28,370	23,662	280,545	9.12	5.12	
60-69		41,537	37,859	388,387	9.73	5.79	13
70-79		57,379	44,152	515,795	9.95	9.39	62
80-89		92,005	52,716	701,960	10.44	10.44	11
90-99		127,521	62,782	973,358	11.15	12.97	24
1700-09		153,015	58,383	1,292,368	11.41	14.26	10

REGIONAL INCOME ESTIMATES UNDER 3 DISCOUNT RATES
1650-1709

(Continued)

	1	2	3	4	5	6	7
	Wage Bill Ƀ/year	Land Payments Ƀ/year	Capital Payments Ƀ/year	Aggregate Income = 1+2+3	Money Income per head	Real Income per head	Percentage Change in col. 6
		r = .10					
1650-59		35,463	29,577	293,553	9.54	5.36	
60-69		51,921	47,324	408,236	10.22	6.08	13
70-79		71,724	55,190	541,178	10.44	9.85	62
80-89		115,006	65,895	738,140	10.98	10.98	11
90-99		159,401	78,478	1,020,934	11.70	13.60	24
1700-09		191,268	72,979	1,345,217	11.88	14.85	09

(a) The range of discount rates were chosen on the basis of English and New World rates found in Sidney Homer, A History of Interest Rates (New Brunswick, N. J.: Rutgers University Press, 1963), pp. 131 and 274-75.

(b) The aggregate wage bill is the average of the two presented in Table 111-11.

(c) Land payments equal the total value of land (Table IV-8) times the interest rate.

(d) Capital payments equal the total value of capital (Table IV-8) times the interest rate.

By combining the returns to land, labor, and capital, we arrive at our final estimate of aggregate regional income, enabling us to quantify the pattern of economic growth in an important section of the English North American colonies. It is immediately apparent from the figures that the New England colonies did experience rapid extensive growth. Between 1650 and 1709 gross regional product in nominal terms rose over four fold while the real product rose over ten fold. On a decennial basis real aggregate output was rising on average at a rate of 61 percent per decade (5 percent per year), a rate which is quite rapid by modern standards.[6]

In terms of real income per head we find that the New England colonists did enjoy substantial efficiency gains. From the beginning to the end of the period the sustained rate of growth was about 1.6 percent annually per person, a rate quite familiar to students of growth subsequent to 1840.[7] The average decade growth rate of 24 percent per person (2.2 percent per annum) mostly reflects the particularily rapid expansion over the seventh and eighth decades of the seventeenth century. From these impressive figures, there can be little doubt that the seventeenth-century New England colonies were experiencing an increase in productivity. Economic growth prior to 1710 was neither slow nor particularily irregular by modern standards; extensive as well as intensive growth did characterize the development of the northern colonies from 1650 to 1709.

Regional Growth in Perspective

Between 1650 and 1709 the New England economy grew from an aggregate output of less than ₤300,000 to more than ₤1,200,000. By themselves, however, these figures have little meaning. Whether or not growth rates were slow or fast or income small or large, depends upon the comparison used. In an attempt to shed light on this "statistical dark age," we shall compare the above with estimates and guesstimates of seventeenth-century income as well as more accurate figures for later dates.

An immediate question that comes to mind is how did the New England incomes compare with those in the mother country? Perhaps the most reliable evidence for the period is Gregory King's English income estimate for 1688. According to him, personal incomes in 1688 amounted to Ѣ7.90 per head.[8] When compared with the colonial figure for the ninth decade, Ѣ9.90, (column 5 Table V-1), it appears that New World incomes were indeed higher. However, a valid comparison would take into account the difference of the currency exchange rate between Old England and New. The difference of exchange between England and the colony at that time amounted to 25 percent, against Massachusetts.[9] Discounting by this amount, we find that colonial incomes had an equivalent English purchasing power of Ѣ7.42. It, therefore, seems safe to conclude that during the ninth decade and probably for most of the last half of the seventeenth century, New Englanders incomes were probably not significantly lower than those of their fellows across the Atlantic.

Estimates such as King's for the west side of the Atlantic are much less definite. Since Raymond W. Goldsmith's testimony before the Joint Economic Committee in 1959,[10] economic historians have done much conjecturing about the path of colonial economic growth. Goldsmith contended:

> There seems little doubt, then, that the average rate of growth of real income per head was much lower than 1-5/8 percent before 1839. If we consider periods of at least 50 years' length, it is questionable that we could find an average rate of growth as high as 1 percent in any one of them.[11]

The evidence presented above is definitely not consistent with Goldsmith's opinion. Indeed, the average growth rate for the sixty-year period between 1650 and 1710 was almost exactly 1-5/8 percent. And even allowing for a 50 percent margin of error in the seventeenth-century estimate, the growth rate was still "as high as 1 percent." These New England figures completely change the picture of colonial growth and emphasize the danger in conjecturing about growth rates before the data has been collected.

Subsequent to the Goldsmith testimony, George Rogers Taylor in his presidential address to the Economic History Association hypothesized,

> that until about 1710 growth was slow, irregular, and not properly measured in percentage terms; that from about 1710 to 1775 the average rate of growth was relatively rapid for a pre-industrial economy (perhaps 1 percent per capita or even a little higher); and that from 1775 until 1840, or possibly a decade earlier, average per capita production showed little if any increase.[12]

Though he believed that the seventeenth century saw extensive growth as evidenced by the rapid population increase, he considered colonial productivity increase to be an eighteenth-century phenomenon. Furthermore, according to Taylor's figures per capita income in 1720 expressed in the prices of the day was roughly £5 or £6. Such conclusions are obviously inconsistent with the findings presented above. New England's economic growth prior to 1710 was not irregular when compared with more recent estimates. Over the sixty-year period decennial averages ranged from as high as 62 percent to as low as 11 percent. This range of decade growth rates implies irregular or cyclical growth. However, comparing the colonial figures with decade rates which varied from 4 percent to 88 percent between 1870 and 1950,[13] we see that colonial fluctuations were no more pronounced than those of a more modern period. Moreover, growth prior to 1710 was secularly rising at a relatively fast rate throughout the period. Indeed, these findings suggest that previous speculation about seventeenth-century efficiency gains were incorrect and that advance from sources such as increasing size of market, improvements in shipping, and more efficient institutions within both markets and governments were larger than formerly expected. When my 1700-09 estimate of approximately £11 per head is compared with Taylor's speculation of £6, it appears that the colonists were significantly better off than he presumed.

Recent articles by Shepard and Walton and McCusker suggest that the rate of eighteenth-century growth was certainly positive.[14] McCusker even ventures to conclude that in Pennsylvania between 1730 and 1770 "the per capita rate of increase in NNP was more like 1.6%"[15] while Shepard and Walton believe that the overall colonial rate was "low when compared with post-1840 rates of growth."[16] Comparing these figures with my estimates, it appears that seventeenth-century New England's growth rate could not have been below the eighteenth-century rate and quite possibly exceeded it.

Comparison of per capita incomes in 1710 and 1840 provides even further insight into the growth rate between the two dates. But first we must transform estimates for the two dates into comparable figures. Using George Chever's estimate that the New England shilling had "an intrinsic value of about 16-2/3 cents,"[17] we can convert the money income per head shown in Table V-1 into dollars and cents. The results can then be compared with the authoritative income studies of Robert Gallman.[18] Taking out the effects of price-level changes, per capita real income in 1700-09 was about $70 (in 1840 prices) as compared to $90 in 1840.[19] According to these figures, during the 140-year period, 1700-1840, real incomes rose only about 28 percent or less than 0.25 percent per annum. Such a growth rate is substantially lower than Gallman's estimate of .3 to .5 percent per year for the same period.[20] If the rate for 1710 to 1840 was indeed this low and the rate for 1700 to 1775 was 1 percent as Shepard and Walton suppose,[21] then perhaps we have not yet truly assessed the costs of the American Revolution.

The levels of real income per head and the rates of growth arrived at here cast much doubt upon the validity and usefulness of previous speculations about the colonial economic development. No claim can be made that the figures developed in this work are without error;[22] nevertheless, allowing for a wide range of error still produces the conclusion that per capita output was rising. During the last half of the seventeenth century, the northern colonies most certainly experienced both extensive and intensive growth. While there is some room to question the magnitude of that growth, the results here indicate that at least during the seventeenth century it was higher than that suggested by Gallman[23] and probably substantial when compared to many modern-day underdeveloped countries. In light of these findings, we can no longer look solely to the nineteenth and twentieth centuries for the keys to economic growth. The relatively rapid seventeenth-century growth of New England undoubtedly laid a strong foundation for future development.

Summary and Conclusions

Prior to this study, economic historians have been able to do little more than speculate about the seventeenth-century growth of the British colonies. Those working in the area have often found the data incomplete and insufficient for the measurement of colonial output. Studies by Taylor,

Gallman, Shepard and Walton, and Alice Hanson Jones have uncovered isolated scraps of evidence but none has systematically quantified the rate of economic growth. Historians of the era have also qualitatively examined the New England economy and its sectors but again none has systematically analyzed the various industries and their relationship to one another.

Within the context of a simple general equilibrium model, this work has presented a framework whereby we can examine shifts in the demand for labor by the three major sectors. Linked through competition in the shipping sector, it has been shown that wages in colonial New England approximated those in the mother country, rising continually throughout the 60 year period.

There has never been much doubt that the colonies experienced extensive growth and this study substantiates such views. By the end of the seventeenth century, settlements covered much of the area which now constitutes the states of Connecticut, Massachusetts, New Hampshire, and Rhode Island. Population during the period was growing at a yearly compound rate of about 2-1/2 percent reaching nearly 100,000 by 1700. Under these conditions, it is a small wonder that real aggregate output for the New England colonies grew over ten fold.

It has traditionally been thought that rapid intensive growth was absent from the colonial scene but the figures here suggest quite the contrary. While it is difficult if not impossible to establish whether the increases were the result of a larger volume of factors per member of the population or of increases in the productivity of the factors, we can be sure that real per capita incomes did grow at least 1 percent per year (compounded).

The findings of this work certainly do suggest economic growth, but caution must be exercised when making inferences about the entire colonial experience from these estimates for the data here is only one small section of the North American colonies. During the early years various sections of the colonies were rather isolated from one another so that growth in one place does not necessarily imply growth elsewhere. The methodology of this study does, however, make it possible to fill in other gaps in this "statistical dark age." Only when similar studies have been conducted for other areas and other dates will we have a complete and representative picture of colonial economic growth.

FOOTNOTES FOR CHAPTER V

1. Taylor, "American Economic Growth before 1840," p. 430.

2. Weeden, Economic and Social History of New England, Vol. I, p. 178.

3. See Chapter II, p. 38.

4. Speaking on the New World interest rates, Sidney Homer says that the history of colonial credit and interest rates is not a history of innovation but rather a history of adaptation." A History of Interest Rates (New Brunswick, N.J.: Rutgers University Press, 1963), p. 274.

5. Ibid., p. 131.

6. Robert E. Gallman, "Gross National Product in the United States, 1834-1909," pp. 7-10.

7. Ibid., p. 9.

8. Pollard and Crossley, The Wealth of Britain, p. 153.

9. Chever, "Commerce of Salem," p. 125.

10. Goldsmith, "Historical and Comparative Rates of Production," pp. 337-361.

11. Ibid., p. 355.

12. Taylor, "American Economic Growth before 1840," p. 429.

13. Robert E. Gallman, "Estimates of American National Product Made Before the Civil War," reprinted in Ralph Andreano, New Views on American Economic Development (Cambridge, Mass.: Schenkman Publishing Co., Inc., 1965), p. 173.

14. James F. Shepherd and Gary M. Walton, "Trade, Distribution, and Economic Growth in Colonial America," Journal of Economic History, XXXII (March 1972), pp. 128-145. John J. McCusker, "Sources of Investment Capital in the Colonial Philadelphia Shipping Industry," Journal of Economic History, XXXII (March 1972), pp. 146-157.

15. McCusker, "Sources of Investment," p. 155.

16. Shepherd and Walton, "Trade, Distribution, and Economic Growth," p. 129.

17. Chever, "Commerce of Salem," p. 121.

18. See Introduction, footnote #2.

19. The price index used for this conversion was Bezanson's "Wholesale Price Index for Philadelphia: 1720 to 1861," Historical Statistics, p. 119. However, since these figures only go back to 1720, I assumed the price index for 1700-09 to be the same as that for 1720. The 1840 per capita income estimate was taken from Gallman, "The Pace and Pattern of American Economic Growth," p. 22.

20. Gallman, "The Pace and Pattern of American Economic Growth," p. 22.

21. Shepherd and Walton, "Trade, Distribution, and Economic Growth," p. 144.

22. For a full discussion of possible bias, see Appendix F.

23. Gallman, "The Pace and Pattern of American Economic Growth," p. 22.

APPENDIX A

STABLE POPULATION MODEL APPLIED

It is necessary to estimate the factors $\mu(a)$, $m(a)$, and $p(a)$ such that they correspond to the historical evidence we can muster. The major problem is to obtain a proxy life table for $p(a)$ since no reliable life table exists for the American colonies. The earliest reliable life table in existence is for England during the years 1838-1854.[1] Fortunately, this life table, which indicated a female life expectancy at age 21 of 60.63, corresponds almost exactly with Greven's historical evidence. He has found that the average age at death for seventeenth-century New England females that had reached the age of 21 was 61.6.[2] We will, therefore, use the English table to estimate $p(a)$ for purposes of determining the relationship between average family size and the natural rate of increase. Alternatively, we could have employed the United Nations Life Tables, selecting the appropriate levels in the same manner. As will become apparent below, it makes no substantive difference which life table is used.

We also do not have a detailed breakdown by age of the proportion of the married female population during the colonial period $\mu(a)$. Fortunately, however, the relationships in which we are interested are not very sensitive to changes in $\mu(a)$. Until recently the accepted view was that the average age of marriage of colonial women was very low, perhaps significantly below the twentieth year. New research has demonstrated that for New England, at least, this was not true. The average age at marriage for New England females for the various locations for which we have information was 21.75 years in the seventeenth century and 21.12 in the eighteenth (see Table A-II). The average age at marriage in 1920 was about the twenty-second year (Table A-1, Column 2). On this basis we rely upon the 1920 marital ratio as a proxy for our period.

The maternity frequency for the colonial period was computed by also selecting the observed frequency for 1920 as is exhibited in Table A-1 and the calculation explained in Table A-1. Following Lotka exactly, the assumption is made that the maternity frequency curve for earlier periods which exhibited higher rates of natural increase would have the same shape except that is would be higher by some constant. That is:

$$1 = \int_0^\infty e^{-ra} \mu(a) \quad m(a) \quad p(a) \; da$$

The k associated with each rate of growth of the population is shown in Table A-3. Thus, had the natural rate of growth during the colonial period been .03 annually, the fecundity during that period would have been 2.605. These results can be expressed as the number of children per married woman and the birthrate that would produce each natural rate of population increase.[3] The relationship between the natural rate of increase (a), the birth rate and the average number of children per married woman is shown in Table II.

TABLE A-1

Age Schedule of Maternity Frequency (Daughters Only)
For "White Females" and "Married White Females"
1920 (Observed) and Females Dying Within Age Groups

(1) Age	(2) Maternity frequency per 100,000 females of all marital states, 1920 m(a)	(3) Percent actually married μ(a)	(4) = (2)/(3) Maternity frequency per 100,000 married females, 1920 m'(a)	(5) Life table deaths d_x 1838-54 p(a)
15-19	2,202	11.5	19,148	2,280
20-24	7,310	50.8	14,390	2,978
25-29	7,480	73.1	10,233	3,157
30-34	5,780	80.3	7,198	3,286
35-39	3,898	81.4	4,789	3,407
40-44	1,552	80.0	1,940	3,544
45-49	172	76.8	224	3,714
50-54	5	72.0	69	3,993

TABLE A-2

Average Age at Marriage
of New England Females

Towns	Period	Average Age	Author
	Seventeenth Century		
Andover	1650-1700	22.8	Greven
Dedham	1640-1690	22.5	Lockridge
Plymouth	1625-1650	20.2	Demos
Plymouth	1650-1675	21.3	Demos
Plymouth	1675-1700	22.3	Demos
New England	Before 1700	21.4	Crum
	Eighteenth Century		
Bristol	Before 1750	20.5	Demos
Bristol	After 1750	21.1	Demos
New England	1700-1744	21.7	Crum
Haverhill	1720-1760	21.7	Higgs-Stettler
Non-Haverhill	1720-1760	20.6	Higgs-Stettler
	Average Seventeenth Century	21.75	
	Average Eighteenth Century	21.12	

SOURCES

Greven, Four Generations, p. 33 or Greven, Philip J., "Family Structure in Seventeenth Century Andover, Massachusetts," William and Mary Quarterly.

Lockridge, Kenneth, "The Population of Dedham, Massachusetts, 1936-1736," Economic History Review, Second series, XII (August 1966), p. 330.

Demos, John, "Notes on the Life in Plymouth Colony," William and Mary Quarterly, Third Series, XXII (1965), p. 275.

Crum, Frederick, S., "The Marriage Rate in Massachusetts," Publ. Am. Statistical Assn., Vol. 4, N.S. #32, December 1895, p. 322-339.

Demos, John, "Families in Colonial Briston, Rhode Island: An Exercise in Historical Demography," William and Mary Quarterly, Third Series, XXV (1968) p. 55.

TABLE A-3

Factor k by Which 1920 Fecundity Would Have to be Multiplied to Give Several Rates of Increase r Also, Constants Employed in Computation

Basis of computation

Mortality as of	1838-54 (English Life Table)
Age schedule of maternity frequency as of	1920
Marital ratio as of	1920

r	
0.0000...............	1.137
+.0050...............	1.308
.0100...............	1.507
.0150...............	1.727
.0200...............	1.987
.0225...............	2.131
.0250...............	2.274
.0275...............	2.440
.0300...............	2.605
.0325...............	2.781
R_o..................	0.880
R_1..................	24.88
R_2..................	743.36
R_3..................	23,363
R_4..................	768,839
α	28.29
β	-44.7
γ	59.46
δ	160.44

FOOTNOTES FOR APPENDIX A

1. Joseph Witaker, An Almanack for the Year of Our Lord 1895 (London: Office 12, Warwick Lane, 1895), pp. 357-58.

2. Greven, Four Generations, p. 196.

3. For a rigorous derivation of this relationship, see Lotka, "The Size of American Families in the Eighteenth Century," p. 29, Appendix A.

APPENDIX B

AVERAGE SIZE OF COMPLETED FAMILY IN MASSACHUSETTS, BY DECADE AND TOWN

County	Hampshire						Worcester	
	Spring-field[a] 1646		Whately[b] 1771		Hadley[c] 1661		North Brookfield[d] 1673	
Decade	No.	(S)	No.	(S)	No.	(S)	No.	(S)
1641-1650	6.9	33	7.8	8	6.8	16	9.33	6
1651-1660	7.8	21	8.8	8	8.9	15	8.0	8
1661-1670	7.56	30	8.7	10	7.6	41	7.4	15
1671-1680	7.0	27	9.1	8	6.43	56	8.2	10
1681-1690	6.84	32	7.85	7	7.05	56	8.37	16
1691-1700	6.85	27	8.71	7	9.4	55	6.69	13
		.72		48		239		68

[a]Burt, Henry M., The First Century of the History of Springfield (Springfield, Mass.: Henry M. Burt, 1898), Vols. I and II.

[b]Crafts, James A., History of the Town of Whately, Massachusetts (Orange, Mass.: D. L. Crandall, Mann's Block, 1899).

[c]Judd, Sylvester, History of Hadley, Massachusetts (Springfield, Mass.: H. R. Hunting & Co., 1905).

[d]Temple, J. I., History of North Brookfield, Massachusetts (Published by the town of North Brookfield, 1887).

APPENDIX B
(Continued)

County / Decade	Middlesex									
	Billerica[e] 1655		Marlborough[f] 1660		Framingham[g] 1700		Newton[h] 1691		Lexington[i] 1713	
	No.	(S)	No.	(S)	No.	(S)	No.	(S)	No.	(S)
1641-1650	8.66	9	6.63	11	7.4	20	7.4	6	7.5	8
1651-1660	8.1	11	9.55	9	8.0	21	11.1	8	8.55	9
1661-1670	8.34	29	7.04	23	7.3	29	7.0	12	8.18	16
1671-1680	6.31	22	5.86	29	7.29	24	7.63	22	6.06	17
1681-1690	7.1	28	6.78	28	6.81	32	7.13	23	7.77	31
1691-1700	7.38	42	7.67	52	6.72	43	5.31	44	7.58	34
		141		152		169		115		115

[e]Hazen, Henry A., History of Billerica, Massachusetts (Boston: A. Williams & Co., 1883).

[f]Hudson, Charles, History of the Town of Marlborough (Boston: T. R. Marvin & Son, 1862).

[g]Temple, J. H., History of Framingham, Massachusetts (Published by the town of Framingham, 1887).

[h]Jackson, Francis, History of the Early Settlement of Newton (Boston: Stacy & Tichardson, 1854).

[i]Hudson, Charles, History of the Town of Lexington, Middlesex County, Massachusetts (Boston and New York: Houghton & Mifflin Co., 1913).

APPENDIX B
(Continued)

County	Suffolk		Plymouth				
	Weymouth[j] 1635		No. Bridgewater[k] 1656		Hingham[l] 1635		Averages
Decade	No.	(S)	No.	(S)	No.	(S)	
1641-1650	5.24	25	9.0	4	6.36	19	6.95
1651-1660	6.32	28	11.0	1	8.05	19	8.10
1661-1670	5.61	34	8.0	2	7.0	31	7.30
1671-1680	5.88	36	6.8	6	6.23	17	6.60
1681-1690	5.63	44	7.2	5	5.10	28	6.80
1691-1700	5.51	37	7.5	4	4.38	21	7.00
		204		22		135	

Total Families = 1580

Total Children = 68,140

Average = 7.13

Standard Deviation = .40

[j]Chamberlin, George Walter, History of Weymouth, Massachusetts (Boston: Wright & Potter, 1923).

[k]Kingman, Bradford, History of North Bridgewater, Massachusetts (Boston: Bradford, Kingman,1886).

[l]History of Town of Hingham, Massachusetts (Published by the town of Hingham, 1893).

APPENDIX C

SAMPLING THE PROBATES ESTATE INVENTORIES

Among the materials yielding quantitative data on colonial American history, probate records are one of the most valuable. Consisting of wills and inventories, these records provide information on residence, occupation, descendents, prices, wealth, etc. Within the last decade in depth studies have tapped this source in an effort to glean a firm understanding of specific counties. More recently, however, Alice Hanson Jones has undertaken a much broader project, attempting to estimate wealth in all of the middle colonies circa 1774.[1] Through these works, both narrow and broad, we have obtained a much better understanding of the pattern of economic growth during our colonial experience.

Much of the data in the present work has also come from the estate inventories. For those not familiar with the estate records, examples are given in Plates C-1 and C-2. It is apparent that from the inventories much can be learned of the Puritan life style. The kinds of household equipment, varieties of food, amount of cloth, quantity of land, etc., provide the historian with an abundance of insight into the colonial environment.[2] But for the purposes of this study the primary contribution of the records was in the estimation of land and capital holdings and the construction of a consumer price index. A time series survey of the probates was to reveal this data, but the question was how to conduct this survey without individually examining each of nearly 3,000 probates.

Following the Jones study, I have surmounted the problem of the huge amount of data available for this large area by randomly sampling the New

PLATE C-1

[illegible] [illegible]

94 Inventory Thomas Hook

An Inventarie of the estate of Thomas Hook deceased taken the twentie six day of Februarie in ye yeare of our Lord God one thousand six hundred seaventy six by John Vindict & John Emms

Imprs. his wearing apparell	03-02-00
It his his bedding	02-00-00
It one cow	04-10-00
It two steeres	03-00-00
It fower sheep	01-12-00
It two swine	02-10-00
It one heiffer	02-00-00
It one 2 yeare old heiffer	01-10-00
It one musquet	01-00-00
It one chest	00-16-00
It one bible	00-05-00
It one sword	00-06-00
more one sword	00-05-00
It ireon work & working tooles	03-00-00
It Indian corne	03-00-00
It a barrell of porke	03-00-00
It other steeres	00-15-00
	31-17-00
It his land	50-00-00
	81-17-00

by us John Emms
John W Vindict
his mark

Rebeckah Binmore made oath to this Inventory in Court Dover Novmr. 1. 1677 J Dudley Assist

PLATE C-2

An Inventory of the estate of Joseph Hubbard of Midleton lately Deceased taken december 1686: (240)

	£	s	d
In wearing apparell Two coats 1=10. One wascoat & drawers & one Leather Suit 1-3-0 one Hat one Shirt drawers & stockings 14s	03	07	00
Two boulsters 2 pillows 3 blankets one payre of Shoes & bed Tick	03	10	00
Three Sheets one flock bed & bowlster one pillow beer	02	06	06
3 old pewter porringers Sucking bottle & one Smale Bason	00	05	00
One brass ketle one brass Skillet & warming pann	02	08	00
One Iron pot & pot Hooks Tramill & Two smothing Irons	00	18	00
One old ketle slice Tongues lamp & one Skillet	00	14	00
Five old Hows 2 axes Hoss chains one sith & tackling	00	18	00
One collor & Hames whiple Tree chaine & bitle rings & 2 wedges	00	09	00
One sickle cow bell old Iron & frying pan 7s	00	07	00
2 Smale barels one powdring Tub churn & keiler	00	10	00
One old sadle & pilion & nayles	01	10	00
2 old Tubbs 2 old keilers one old Barell	00	04	00
2 bedsteds & curtains	01	04	00
3 milk bowles & other smale wooden ware	00	06	00
2 meal Seives butter Tubb one bucket 2 payles	00	06	06
6 Spoons one Tunnill one chest one box one cubboard	00	13	00
One Gun one sword & belt & other ammunition	01	07	00
4li of Sheeps wooll & 8 pound of yarne	01	05	00
2 Napkins 3 Towels one bible & sermon Booke	00	08	00
2 Spining wheels 3 chayres Hamer & glass botle	00	07	00
Six pound of cotton wooll & halfe bushell of Flax seed	00	10	00
One old Hors one mare one 2 year old Coalt	08	00	00
Two cows & two Two year old heifers — 11li			
Eleven Sheep one Sowe & 3 pigs	06	00	00
Eight bushell of meslin & 20 bushels of Indian corne	03	18	00
Dweling house & litle Shop & Barne	22	00	00
Home lott six acres & a halfe	30	00	00
woodland 95 acres 10li one parcell more west from the Towne 118 acres	16	00	00
wood land on the east side the great River 250 acres 6li	06	00	00
Two acres & 3 roods of meadow at wongunck & one at pessen chag	13	00	00
There was omitted at First one cutting knife & Hinges Two old forks & meal sack all — 9s	139	11	00

Legacies Joseph Hubbard 15 years Robert Hubbard 13 years

George Hubbard — 11 years John Hubbard 8 years

Elizabeth Hubbard 3 years old

There is also a legacy by captn Wetts his will To Joseph Hubbard

Taken by us Midleton december 86: Nath: White

Robert: Warner

England inventories. In constructing this sample I have tried to avoid statistical bias or at least predict its influence when it does occur. But the very nature of the surviving inventories makes it impossible to completely avoid the bias problem. For example, a major possibility of bias lies in the fact that the existing records do not constitute 100% of the original estates. Because some records have been destroyed or are illegible and because some estates were never probated, estimates of surviving inventories range from 25% (Davisson) to 50% (Lockridge) of the original records. With no evidence to the contrary, it is assumed that the pattern of wealth shown by the existing records is not different from that of the original decedent population.

In order to make reasonably accurate inferences about the true wealth pattern of all decedents in seventeenth-century New England, the surviving records were randomly sampled at a single stage using counties as the sampling unit. With the exception of New Hampshire where records have been preserved at the colony level, counties were responsible for the collection and preservation of estate records making them the most natural subdivision of the material. To further reduce data requirements the possibility of a two stage sample, drawing first from the population of counties and second from the decedents within each chosen county, was considered. However, for the purposes of this time series survey the first stage proves unmanageable for during the course of the century new counties are continually being formed and old ones are often consolidated.[3] Hence, the data contained herein was drawn by individual from each sampling unit. This technique also insured information for each county.

The question of how large a sample should be drawn from each county depends upon the trade off between accuracy and the cost of collecting data.

In equation form the size of the sample can be expressed as

$$n_0 = \frac{t^2 S^2}{d^2}$$

where t is the value of the normal deviate corresponding to the desired level of confidence, S^2 is the variance of total wealth per individual, and d is the chosen margin of error around the mean.[4] This equation will estimate n_0 unless n_0/N, where N = the total population, is large, in which case we compute n as

$$n = \frac{n_0}{1 + n_0/N}$$

Since the equations contain unknown parameters of the population, it was necessary to conduct a pilot study. To do so I examined the Digest of Early Connecticutt Probate Records[5] which contained total values of seventeenth-century estates. From this survey it became apparent that the variance of wealth holdings was quite high thus increasing the possibility of sampling error. For example during the decade of the 1650's average wealth was approximately 283₤ while the standard error was 357. To achieve 80% accuracy given these parameters nearly 60% of the probates must be examined. The simplest way of increasing the accuracy is to increase the sample size, but this also raises the cost of obtaining the sample. Alternatively, since the sampling error is a direct function of the variability per unit, it is possible to diminish the sample size and improve accuracy by reducing variability. The easiest method of accomplishing this task is stratification, i.e., by dividing the data into homogeneous blocks and sampling within each stratum, the variance in each sub-population can be reduced.

Again, on the basis of the pilot study of Connecticutt, decedents were grouped according to whether their total wealth was greater than or less than 200£. Although it might appear better to classify the inventories into even smaller, more homogeneous groups, costs of such stratification made the aforementioned groups most desirable. The parameters of each stratum and the sample size necessary for 80% confidence for the Connecticutt inventories during the 1650's are shown in Table C-1. The choice of 80% confidence was made mainly on the basis of time costs of collecting the wealth data.

TABLE C-1

Connecticut Inventories
1650-1659

	Total Wealth	
	Less than 200£	Greater than 200£
N	41	27
Mean Wealth	84.24	577
Standard error	52.17	419
$n_0 = \frac{t^2 s^2}{d^2}$	16	21
$n = n_0/1 + n_0/N$	12	12

From the data shown in Table C-1 and similar surveys for other decades, it was decided that the sample would include approximately 30% of all the inventories less than 200£ and 45% of all the inventories greater than 200£.

With this goal in mind, I proceeded to collect as many inventories as possible. Given the expanse of nearly 3,000 miles between my location at the University of Washington and the seat of the actual probates, I was forced to rely entirely upon published or micro-filmed sources.[6] The dates for which inventories are available and their sources are listed in Table C-2.

From this table important sources of sample bias become immediately apparent. The first results from the dearth of information during the 1650's. While there is some possibility that additional information might be available from original courthouse sources, it seems likely that a majority of the early records have not survived. This opens the door for potential bias. Nonetheless, since Essex County, the only county with available probates for the 1650's, claimed a major portion of the inhabitants during this decade, it is quite possible that Essex decedents were indeed representative of New England as a whole. A second gap in the records also involves Essex County, for her probates run only through 1683. Since the county was such an important commercial center, we would expect its exclusion from the sample to introduce downward bias in our estimates of commercial wealth, shipping capital, labor engaged in the commercial sector, etc. Wherever relevant this bias must be noted and corrected if possible. A final source of bias exists due to the fact that certain counties have no records whatsoever. For example, the probate records of Suffolk County which includes Boston as well as those of Plymouth and Rhode Island Colonies were not available in sufficient number to be included in the sample. The potential bias will again depend upon the economic profile of the various locations. Qualitatively we would expect the exclusion of Suffolk to bias downward commercially related estimates and the exclusion of Plymouth and Rhode Island to bias downward agriculturally related estimates.

TABLE C-2

Decade	Established Counties and Colonies	Available Records
1650-59	New Hampshire Colony Essex, Mass. Middlesex, Mass. Plymouth Colony Suffolk, Mass. Old Norfolk, Mass. Rhode Island Colony New Haven Colony Connecticut Colony	Essex[a] Hartford[b] (Abstracts)
1660-69		Essex Hartford (Abstracts) New Hampshire[c] New Haven[d]
1670-79	Hampshire, Mass.	Essex Hartford (Abstracts) New Hampshire New Haven Fairfield[e]
1680-89		Hartford Co.[f] New Hampshire New Haven Fairfield
1690-99	Barnstable, Mass.) Established from Bristol, Mass.) Plymouth Plymouth, Mass.) County Dukes, Mass. Nantucket, Mass.	Hartford New Hampshire New Haven Fairfield Bristol[g]
1700-09		Same

Sources:

[a]George Francis Dow, ed., The Probate Records of Essex County Massachusetts, 1635-1681, (Salem, Massachusetts, 1916-1920), 3 Vols.

[b]Charles William Manwaring, ed., A Digest of Early Connecticut Records (Hartford, Conn.: R. S. Peck and Co., 1904-1906).

[c]New Hampshire Province Probate Records 1655-1713 (filmed by the Geneological Society of the Church of Jesus Christ of Latter-day Saints), Vols. 1-3.

Sources (Continued):

[d]Town of New Haven, Connecticut, Register of Probate Records 1647-1712 (filmed by the Geneological Society of the Church of Jesus Christ of Latter-day Saints), Vols. 1-3.

[e]Town of Fairfield, Connecticut, Register of Probate Records 1648-1750 (filmed by the Geneological Society of the Church of Jesus Christ of Latter-day Saints), Vols. 1-5.

[f]Town of Hartford, Connecticut, Register of Probate Records 1677-1710 (filmed by the Geneological Society of the Church of Jesus Christ of Latter-day Saints), Vols. 4-6.

[g]Bristol County, Commonwealth of Massachusetts, Register of Probate Records, 1687-1710 (filmed by the Geneological Society of the Church of Jesus Christ of Latter-day Saints), Vols. 1-2.

Before drawing the random sample from the population of probate records, it was necessary to stratify the inventories according to total wealth. To ensure a decennial time series, the individuals were grouped by decade of death. The count of inventories within each stratum and the number sampled are shown in Table C-3. To facilitate sampling, decedents within a sub-group were first numbered sequentially. The appropriate number of observations was then drawn by consulting a random numbers table. If upon examination an inventory was incomplete or was illegible, it was not included in the sample and no provision for substitute inventory was made. From these inventories estimates of wealth, land, and capital holding in seventeenth-century New England were made.

TABLE C-3

SIZE OF THE INVENTORY SAMPLE BY COUNTY

	Actual no. of inventories less than 200 (1)	no. sampled (2)	Actual no. of inventories greater than 200 (3)	no. sampled (4)
1650-59				
Essex	48	14	35	16
1660-69				
Essex	126	35	69	32
New Haven	46	13	21	9
New Hampshire	16	5	13	6
1670-79				
Essex	230	65	122	59
New Haven	54	15	28	12
New Hampshire	41	12	20	9
Fairfield	34	10	29	13
1680-89				
New Haven	75	23	71	31
New Hampshire	26	8	11	5
Fairfield	64	17	61	27
Hartford	106	33	98	44
1690-99				
New Haven	79	24	92	41
New Hampshire	42	13	25	11
Fairfield	83	25	82	35
Hartford	107	32	120	47
Bristol	33	10	34	15
1700-09				
New Haven	75	23	72	32
New Hampshire	28	9	8	4
Fairfield	58	17	65	30
Hartford	88	16	82	21
Bristol	54	16	45	20
TOTAL	1,513	435	1,203	519

FOOTNOTES FOR APPENDIX C

1. Jones, "Middle Colonies."

2. For the use of these records in constructing a picture of seventeenth-century New England, see Rutman, Husbandmen of Plymouth.

3. In the Alice Hanson Jones study cluster sampling at the county level was possible since her major interest was in cross section estimates for the year 1774. See Jones, "Middle Colonies," p. 15.

4. William G. Cochran, Sampling Techniques, pp. 56, 57.

5. Compiled by Charles W. Manwaring, Digest of Early Connecticutt Probate Records, Vol. I, 1635-1700 (Hartford: F. S. Peck and Co., Printers, 1904).

6. I wish to thank the Geneological Society of the Church of Jesus Christ of Latter-day Saints for the use of their micro-films of probate records.

APPENDIX D
WEALTH, LAND, AND CAPITAL BY ESTATE SIZE

TABLE D-1

WEALTH[(a)]

(Ŀ)

Decade	Essex			Bristol			New Haven			Fairfield		
	Less than 200Ŀ	Greater than 200Ŀ	Weighted Average	Less than 200Ŀ	Greater than 200Ŀ	Weighted Average	Less than 200Ŀ	Greater than 200Ŀ	Weighted Average	Less than 200Ŀ	Greater than 200Ŀ	Weighted Average
1650-59	88.51	319.38	185.86									
1660-69	89.72	374.48	190.48				118.14	453.19	223.15			
1670-79	63.23	698.74	283.49				84.98	448.93	222.91	71.54	438.18	240.31
1680-89							93.52	443.13	258.61	68.26	445.62	252.41
1690-99				99.18	405.62	254.68	89.96	515.45	318.87	102.08	517.36	308.46
1700-09				89.39	400.20	230.66	97.16	469.17	316.77	91.63	430.16	273.35

Decade	Hartford			New Hampshire			New England
	Less than 200Ŀ	Greater than 200Ŀ	Weighted Average	Less than 200Ŀ	Greater than 200Ŀ	Weighted Average	Average
1650-59	(81.27)	(502.13)	(249.61)				217.73
1660-69	(87.45)	(608.18)	(325.86)	99.87	515.78	286.31	256.45
1670-79	(81.77)	(550.23)	(288.57)	59.54	696.72	268.45	260.75
1680-89	78.72	605.58	331.81	123.72	666.62	285.12	281.98
1690-99	87.82	555.90	335.26	95.80	467.13	234.35	290.32
1700-09	83.78	409.76	241.01	97.17	469.17	179.82	282.07

(a) For the weights used to compute the weighted average, see Appendix C, Table C-3)

TABLE D-2

LAND

(Ѣ)

Decade	Essex: Less than 200Ѣ	Essex: Greater than 200Ѣ	Essex: Weighted Average	Bristol: Less than 200Ѣ	Bristol: Greater than 200Ѣ	Bristol: Weighted Average	New Haven: Less than 200Ѣ	New Haven: Greater than 200Ѣ	New Haven: Weighted Average	Fairfield: Less than 200Ѣ	Fairfield: Greater than 200Ѣ	Fairfield: Weighted Average
1650-59	21.00	112.95	59.64									
1660-69	42.90	119.50	95.48				37.92	95.43	55.94			
1670-79	28.07	430.81	167.65				25.70	124.12	59.30	30.45	238.18	126.07
1680-89							49.20	283.60	162.24	27.56	285.51	153.43
1690-99				48.17	246.68	148.90	37.74	308.50	183.41	44.01	347.01	194.59
1700-09				40.47	269.94	144.77	41.67	323.17	179.54	48.44	279.81	170.70

Decade	Hartford: Less than 200Ѣ	Hartford: Greater than 200Ѣ	Hartford: Weighted Average	New Hampshire: Less than 200Ѣ	New Hampshire: Greater than 200Ѣ	New Hampshire: Weighted Average	New England: Average
1650-59	35.68	324.40	151.17[a]				105.40
1660-69	39.57	390.15	200.08	52.80	212.00	124.16	118.91
1670-79	36.00	354.22	176.47	18.17	355.78	128.86	131.67
1680-89	33.91	398.24	208.93	35.19	252.90	99.91	156.37
1690-99	33.79	347.91	199.84	56.31	195.66	108.30	167.00
1700-09	48.06	282.34	161.06	63.59	299.88	116.09	154.43

[a]For the regressions used to compute Hartford Land holdings prior to 1680, see Table IV-2

TABLE D-3

CAPITAL
(Ѣ)

Decade	Essex			Bristol			New Haven			Fairfield		
	Less than 200Ѣ	Greater than 200Ѣ	Weighted Average	Less than 200Ѣ	Greater than 200Ѣ	Weighted Average	Less than 200Ѣ	Greater than 200Ѣ	Weighted Average	Less than 200Ѣ	Greater than 200Ѣ	Weighted Average
1650-59	41.38	168.74	94.79									
1660-69	22.05	129.20	59.96				46.94	250.51	110.74			
1670-79	20.70	224.35	91.28				26.10	234.35	97.21	22.66	120.29	67.60
1680-89							20.90	92.71	55.82	25.15	94.56	59.02
1690-99				26.34	105.96	66.74	23.73	115.08	72.88	26.62	99.87	63.02
1700-09				27.53	80.66	51.68	19.90	123.83	70.80	17.11	86.31	53.68

Decade	Hartford			New Hampshire			New England
	Less than 200Ѣ	Greater than 200Ѣ	Weighted Average	Less than 200Ѣ	Greater than 200Ѣ	Weighted Average	Average
1650-59	21.49	107.10	55.73[a]				(75.26)
1660-69	22.91	135.74	74.57	10.46	266.60	125.81	(92.77)
1670-79	21.61	120.09	65.08	18.39	254.07	95.66	(83.37)
1680-89	20.54	127.64	71.99	38.25	202.74	87.15	68.49
1690-99	25.71	137.97	85.05	29.05	123.45	64.27	70.39
1700-09	18.77	68.84	42.92	21.68	73.06	33.10	50.44

[a]For the regression used to compute Hartford capital holdings prior to 1680, see Table IV-2.

APPENDIX E

THE COMMODITY PRICE INDEX

For any time series income analysis, it is imperative that we examine changes in the price level if statements are to be made about real income. Not unlike other data for the colonial era, price series are nearly nonexistent. Some wholesale price indicies do extend back through the eighteenth century, but none include the seventeenth century.[1] In his study of Essex County probate records, William Davisson attempts to construct a consumer and producer price index, but they cover a relatively short period of time, 1640-1682, and have several drawbacks.[2] For example, Davisson includes many heterogeneous items such as sheets, skillets, hats, etc. for which we cannot compare price and quantity. Also, he makes no attempt to weigh the items in the index. To avoid these problems and provide an additional source of price information, I have constructed an alternative commodity price index.

To construct this price index, I have used the information found in the previously discussed[3] New England estate inventories. Prices were taken mostly from the random sample used to collect the wealth data. However, in cases where an insufficient number of observations were available, additional inventories were consulted. A pilot study of the price data revealed a much smaller variance making it possible to obtain higher confidence with fewer observations.

A major problem with inventory prices is heterogeneity of commodities. Seldom do the inventories describe beds, chairs, or other household items in sufficient detail to allow one to compare prices and quantities. There is no way of telling whether durable items were new or old and this would undoubtedly affect the per unit value. Only with a large number of observations could we be sure of obtaining the "average" price of such items. For this reason, many of the inventoried possessions are not included in the index. Reasonable homogeneity was a prerequisite for inclusion.

The second major drawback of this price source is the lack of value and quantity designation. Many different items were grouped together and a value then assigned to the entire group. Also, commodities were listed under a plural heading (e.g., cattle, horses, sheep, etc.) with no clue as to the actual quantity. In these cases, it was impossible to obtain per unit values and the observations were not used.

During the seventeenth century by far the largest portion of an individual's consumption expenditures went to food and clothing. Hence, an index including these items should reflect the overall consumer price index. Commodities shown in Table E-1 were chosen because of the homogeneous qualities, their frequency in the inventories, and their importance in the consumption bundle. The agricultural items including livestock and grains were produced mainly in the northern colonies; the manufactured textiles, on the other hand, were mostly imported from the mother country.

The prices were collected for each county by decade and simple averages are presented in Table E-1. Across counties prices differed very little providing strong evidence that a New England market did exist. Distinct trends can be seen in the data. Corn and wheat prices remained relatively stable over the sixty-year period while livestock prices showed a general decline throughout the era. Textile (manufacturing) prices exhibit no distinct trend during the last half of the seventeenth century but do tend to move with one another. Comparing the foodstuff and textile series, it is quite clear that agricultural prices were declining relative to manufacturing.

The final price index is a weighted average of the decade averages. Weights were chosen on the basis of the percent of total wealth held in each commodity and allowed to vary between decades. On average, agricultural commodities constituted over 85 percent of the index. The base of 1680-89 was chosen to facilitate comparison with wealth and income estimates for England in 1688. The resulting commodity price index declines continually between 1650 and 1709 with the largest decade decline occurring between the 1660's and 1670's. This index was used to deflate all estimates given in real terms.

TABLE E-1

INDEX OF COMMODITY PRICES
1650-1709

Base: 1680-89 = 100

	Horses Ł/head	Oxen Ł/head	Sheep Ł/head	Swine Ł/head	Cattle Ł/head	Corn Ł/bushel	Wheat Ł/bushel
1650-59	11.6	6.58	1.03	.97	4.24	.14	.24
1660-69	8.52	6.82	.51	.84	4.11	.14	.24
1670-79	3.53	5.54	.42	.74	3.60	.14	.23
1680-89	3.30	5.75	.45	.82	3.46	.13	.24
1690-99	3.04	5.21	.46	.75	3.27	.13	.26
1700-09	2.86	5.39	.47	.71	3.44	.13	.28

	Yarn Ł/yard	Broad Cloth Ł/yard	Cotton Ł/yard	Kersey & Serge Ł/yard	Weighted Average	Price Index
1650-59	.07	.68	.14	.30	4.62	1.78
1660-69	.13	.71	.16	..35	4.35	1.68
1670-79	.11	.66	.17	.27	2.74	1.06
1680-89	.11	.56	.16	.28	2.59	1.00
1690-99	.13	.92	.17	.36	2.24	.86
1700-09	.12	.72	.18	.32	2.08	.80

FOOTNOTES FOR APPENDIX E

1. See the Warren and Pearson and the Bezanson wholesale price indices in _Historical Statistics_, pp. 115-16 and 119-120.

2. William I. Davisson,"Essex County Price Trends,"_EIHC_, April 1967, pp. 114-185.

3. See Appendix C.

APPENDIX F

POSSIBLE SOURCES OF BIAS

Any quantitative historical study is always subject to some margin of error due to inherent biases in the data or random sampling errors. Such errors, however, do not negate the usefulness of the quantitative evidence, for if the direction error can be predicted we can still make qualified statements from the data. Without knowing the exact population parameters, it is impossible to determine the random sampling error. We can only be sure that on the average it will decrease as the number in the sample increases. Bias in the data, on the other hand, will not change regardless of sample size and will be a direct function of the quality of sources, the methods of selection, and the techniques of transforming the original evidence. Let us examine the evidence in this work for possible biases and attempt to discern their direction.

Determining the seventeenth-century New England population required the estimation of several demographic parameters. Estimates of such parameters as proportion of married females, maternity frequency, and probability of living to a given age all conformed to the known demographic evidence. Also, the final estimate of the population growth rate was not very sensitive to changes in these parameters. The average size of completed family, however, is an important source of potential error. Since the selected families all came from Massachusetts towns, it was necessary to assume that these are representative of New England as a whole. The validity of this assumption will only be known when more is known about the other colonies. At this point we can only refer to Table III-2 and recognize that if our estimate of average size of completed family is too large, we have indeed over-estimated the population growth rate.

Turning to the wealth estimates, it was necessary to assume that the surviving records are representative of all probate-type decedents, that the proportion of surviving records was about twenty-five percent, and that the value of nonprobate-type estates was about one-half the probate-type. Again, there is no way of testing the validity of these assumptions to determine the direction of bias or the margin of error. Such assumptions can only be defended on the basis of their consistency with existing knowledge.

To the extent that biases do exist, the absolute values of the figures may be in error. However, if the direction of the bias remains constant over the period, we can maintain our faith in the estimated rates of growth. For example, if per capita income is over-estimated in 1650 and 1700 by fifty percent, the rate of change between the two dates will not be affected. For all the potential sources of bias discussed above, there is no reason to believe that the direction or magnitude of bias shifted. Therefore, the growth rates should stand upon solid ground.

BIBLIOGRAPHY

Primary Sources

Connecticut, Town of Fairfield, Register of Probate Records, Vols. 1-5, 1648-1750. Filmed by the Geneological Society of The Church of Jesus Christ of Latter-day Saints.

Connecticut, Town of Hartford, Register of Probate Records, Vols. 4-6, 1677-1710. Filmed by the Geneological Society of the Church of Jesus Christ of Latter-day Saints.

Connecticut, Town of New Haven, Register of Probate Records, Vols. 1-3, 1647-1712. Filmed by the Geneological Society of the Church of Jesus Christ of Latter-day Saints.

A Digest of the Early Connecticut Records, compiled by Charles William Manwaring (Hartford: R. S. Peck & Company, 1904-06).

Massachusetts, Bristol County Commonwealth of, Register of Probate Records, Vols. 1 and 2, 1687-1710. Filmed by the Geneological Society of the Church of Jesus Christ of Latter-day Saints.

New Hampshire, Provence of, Register of Probate Records, Vols. 1-3, 1655-1713. Filmed by the Geneological Society of the Church of Jesus Christ of Latter-day Saints.

The Probate Records of Essex County, Massachusetts (1635-1681), 3 Vols., edited by George Francis Dow (Salem, Mass.: 1916-1920).

The Public Records of the Colony of Connecticut 1636-1665 (Hartford: Brown and Parsons, 1850).

Records of the Colony and Plantation of New Haven, 2 Vols. (Hartford: Case, Tiffany and Co., 1857-58).

Secondary Sources

Adams, Herbert B. "Common Fields in Salem," Essex Institute Historical Collection, XIX (1882).

_____. "Salem Meadows, Woodland, and Town Neck," Essex Institute Historical Collection, XX (1883).

Adams, James Truslow. The Founding of New England. Boston: Little Brown, 1939.

Akagi, Roy H. The Town Proprietors of the New England Colonies. Philadelphia: Press of the University of Pennsylvania, 1924.

Albion, Robert G. Forests and Sea Power. Cambridge, Mass.: Harvard University Press, 1926.

Andrews, Charles M. River Towns of Connecticut, A Study of Wethersfield, Hartford, and Windsor. Baltimore: Johns Hopkins Press, 1889.

Bailyn, Bernard. The New England Merchants in the Seventeenth Century. New York: Harper & Row, Publishers, 1955.

Bailyn, Bernard and Bailyn, Lotte. Massachusetts Shipping 1697-1774. Cambridge, Mass.: Harvard University Press, 1959.

Barnes, Viola Florence. "Land Tenure in English Colonial Charters of the Seventeenth Century," In Essays in Colonial History Presented to Charles McLean Andrews by his Students. New Haven: Yale University Press, 1931.

Beer, George Louis. The Origins of the British Colonial System 1578-1660. New York: Peter Smith, 1933.

_____. The Old Colonial System 1660-1754, 2 Vols. New York: Peter Smith, 1933.

Bidwell, Percy Wells, and Falconer, John I. History of Agriculture in the Northern United States 1620-1860. Washington, D.C.: Carnegie Institution of Washington, 1925.

Bjork, Gordon C. "The Weaning of the American Economy: Independence, Market Changes, and Economic Development," Journal of Economic History, XXIV (December, 1964).

Bridenbaugh, Carl. Vexed and Troubled Englishmen 1590-1642. New York: Oxford University Press, 1968.

Buffington, Arthur H. "New England and the Western Fur Trade, 1629-1676," Colonial Society of Mass. Publications, XVIII (1915-1916).

Chambers, Edward J. and Gordon, Donald F. "Primary Products and Economic Growth An Empirical Measurement," Journal of Political Economy, LXXIV (August, 1966).

Chever, George F. "Some Remarks on the Commerce of Salem from 1626-1740," Essex Institute Historical Collection, I (1859).

Clark, Charles E. The Eastern Frontier 1610-1763. New York: Alfred A. Knopf, 1970.

David, Paul. A. "New Light on a Statistical Dark Age: U.S. Real Product Growth before 1840," American Economic Review. 57 (May, 1967).

_____. "The Growth of Real Product in the United States Before 1840: New Evidence and Controlled Conjectures," Journal of Economic History, 27 (June, 1967).

Davis, Lance, et al. American Economic Growth An Economist's History of the United States. New York: Harper and Row, Publishers, 1972.

Davisson, William I. "Essex County Wealth Trends: Wealth and Economic Growth in 17th Century Massachusetts," Essex Institute Historical Collections, CIII (October, 1967).

_____. "Essex County Price Trends: Money and Markets in 17th Century Massachusetts," Essex Institute Historical Collections, CII (April, 1967).

Davisson, William I., and Dugan, Dennis J. "Land Precedents in Essex County, Massachusetts," Essex Institute Historical Collection, CVI (October, 1970).

Demos, John. A Little Commonwealth, Family Life in Plymouth Colony. New York: Oxford University Press, 1970.

Dorfman, Joseph. The Economic Mind in American Civilization 1606-1865. New York: Augustus M. Kelley Publishers, 1966.

Douglass, William. A Summary, Historical and Political, of the First Planting, Progressive Improvements, and the Present State of the Present State of the British Settlements in North-America, 2 Vols. London: R. & J. Dodsley, 1760.

Dyson, Verne. Anecodotes and Events in Long Island History. Port Washington, New York: Ira J. Friedman, Inc., 1969.

Egleston, Melville. "Land System of the New England Colonies," Johns Hopkins University Studies in Historical and Political Science, XI-XII, 4th Series.

Farnie, D.A. "The Commercial Empire of the Atlantic 1607-1783," Economic History Review, XV, 2nd Series (December, 1962).

Felt, Joseph B. Annals of Salem. Salem, Mass.: W. & S. V. Ives, (1845).

_____. "Statistics of Population in Massachusetts," American Statistical Association Collections, I (1845).

Fogel, Robert and Engerman, Stanley, ed. The Reinterpretation of American Economic History. New York: Harper & Row, Publishers, 1971.

Gallman, Robert E. "Commodity Output, 1839-1899." In Trends in the American Economy in the Nineteenth Century. Conference on Research in Income and Wealth, Studies in Income and Wealth, Vol. 24. Princeton, N.J.: Princeton University Press, 1960.

_____. "Gross National Product in the United States, 1834-1909." In Output, Employment and Productivity in the U.S. After 1800. Conference on Research in Income and Wealth, Studies in Income and Wealth, Vol. 30. Princeton, N.J.: Princeton University Press, 1966.

_____. "Trends in the Size Distribution of Wealth in the Nineteenth Century: Some Speculations." In Six Papers on the Size Distribution of Wealth and Income. Conference on Research in Income and Wealth, Studies in Income and Wealth, Vol. 23. New York: Columbia University Press, 1969.

_____. "Estimates of American National Product Made Before the Civil War," Economic Development and Cultural Change (April, 1961).

Gallman, Robert E., and Howle, E. S. "The Structure of U.S. Wealth in the Nineteenth Century." Paper presented at the 1966 meeting of the Southern Economic Association, Atlanta, Georgia.

Goldsmith, Raymond W. Historical and Comparative Rates of Production, Productivity and Prices. Hearings before the Joint Economic Committee, 86th Cong., 1st Sess., 2, April 7, 1959. Washington, D.C.: Government Printing Office, 1959.

_____. "The Growth of Reproducible Wealth of the United States of America from 1805-1950." In Income and Wealth of United States: Trends and Structure, edited by Simon Kuznets. International Association for Research in Income and Wealth, Income and Wealth Series, Vol. 2. Baltimore: Johns Hopkins Press, 1952.

Greven, Philip J. Four Generations: Population, Land and Family in Colonial Andover, Massachusetts. Ithaca, N.Y.: Cornell University Press, 1970.

Harris, Marshall. Origins of the Land Tenure System in the United States. Ames: Iowa State College Press, 1953.

Henretta, James A. "Economic Development and Social Structure in Colonial Boston," William and Mary Quarterly. 25, 3rd Series (January, 1965).

Hilkey, Charles J. Legal Developments in Colonial Massachusetts 1630-1686. New York: Columbia University Press, 1910. Also printed in Columbia University Studies in History, Economics, and Public Law, XXXVII, #2.

Hoenach, Stephen A. "Historical Censuses and Estimates of Wealth in the United States." In Measuring the Nation's Wealth, George Washington University, Wealth Inventory Planning Study. NBER Studies in Income and Wealth, Vol. 29. Washington, D.C.: Government Printing Office, 1964.

Homer, Sidney. A History of Interest Rates. New Brunswick, N.J.: Rutgers University Press, 1963.

Hooker, Roland M. "The Colonial Trade of Connecticut." In Publications of the Tercentenary Commission of the State of Connecticut. New Haven: 1936.

Innis, Harold A. The Cod Fisheries. New Haven: Yale University Press, 1940.

Jernegan, Marcus Wilson. Laboring and Dependent Classes in Colonial America 1607-1783. Chicago: University of Chicago Press, 1931.

Johnson, E. A. J. "Some Evidence of Merchantilism in Massachusetts Bay," New England Quarterly, I (July, 1928).

Jonas, Manfred. "The Wills of the Early Settlers of Essex County, Massachusetts," Essex Institute Historical Collection, XCVI (July, 1960).

Jones, Alice Hanson. "Wealth Estimates for the American Middle Colonies, 1774," Economic Development and Cultural Change, 18 (July, 1970).

_____. "Wealth Estimates for the New England Colonies, about 1774," Journal of Economic History, XXXII (March, 1972).

Koch, Donald W. "Income Distribution and Political Structure in 17th Century Salem, Massachusetts," Essex Institute Historical Collections, CV (January, 1969).

Lampman, Robert J. The Share of Top Wealth-Holders in National Wealth, 1922-1956. NBER Study No. 74. Princeton, N.J.: Princeton University Press, 1962.

Leach, Douglas E. The Northern Colonial Frontier 1607-1763. New York: Holt, Rinehart and Winston, 1966.

Lebergott, Stanley. "Labor Force and Employment 1800-1960." In Output, Employment, and Productivity in the United States after 1800. Conference on Research in Income and Wealth, Studies in Income and Wealth, Vol. 30. Princeton, N.J.: Princeton University Press, 1966.

_____. Manpower in Economic Growth. New York: McGraw Hill Book Co., 1964.

_____. "Population Change and the Supply of Labor." In Demographic and Economic Change in Developed Countries. Princeton, N.J.: Princeton University Press, 1960.

Liversage, Vincent. Land Tenure in the Colonies. Cambridge: Cambridge University Press, 1945.

Lockridge, Kenneth. A New England Town--The First Hundred Years: Dedham Massachusetts, 1636-1736. New York: W. W. Norton & Co., Inc., 1970.

_____. "Land, Population and the Evolution of New England Society 1630-1790," Past and Present, 39 (1968).

Lotka, Alfred J. Elements of Physical Biology. Baltimore: Williams & Wilkins Co., 1925.

McCusker, John J. "Sources of Investment Capital in the Colonial Philadelphia Shipping," Journal of Economic History, XXXII (March, 1972).

Main, Jackson T. The Social Structure of Revolutionary America. Princeton, N.J.: Princeton University Press, 1965.

Malone, Joseph J. Pine Trees and Politics. Seattle, Washington: University of Washington Press, 1964.

Martin, Robert F. National Income in the United States, 1799-1938. National Industrial Conference Board Studies, no. 241. New York: National Industrial Conference Board, 1939.

Mathews, Lois Kimball. The Expansion of New England. New York: Russell & Russell Inc., 1962.

Moloney, Francis X. The Fur Trade in New England 1620-1676. Namden, Conn.: Archon Books, 1967.

Morris, Richard B. Government and Labor in Early America. New York: Harper & Row, Publishers, 1946.

Nash, Gray B. Class and Society in Early America. Englewood Cliffs, N.J.: Prentice Hall, 1970.

North, Douglass C. "Early National Income Estimates of the United States," Economic Development and Cultural Change, 9 (April, 1961).

_____. Growth and Welfare in the American Past. Englewood Cliffs, N.J.: Prentice Hall, Inc., 1966.

_____. "Sources of Productivity Change in Shipping, 1600-1850," Journal of Political Economy, 76 (Sept./Oct., 1968).

Perley, Sidney. "Records of the Proprietors of Common Land in Boxford, 1683-1710," Essex Institute Historical Collections, XLII (1906).

Powell, Sumner Chilton. Puritan Village. Garden City, N.Y.: Doubleday & Company, Inc., 1965.

Rossiter, W. S. A Century of Population Growth from the First Census of the United States to the Twelfth 1790-1900. U.S. Bureau of the Census Monograph. Washington, D.C.: Government Printing Office, 1909.

Rutman, Darrett B. "Governor Winthrop's Garden Crop: The Significance of Agriculture in the Early Commerce of Massachusetts Bay," William and Mary Quarterly, XX, 3rd Series (July, 1963).

_____. Husbandmen of Plymouth. Boston: Beacon Press, 1967.

_____. Winthrop's Boston Portrait of a Puritan Town, 1630-1649. Chapel Hill, N.C.: University of North Carolina Press, 1965.

Sachs, William S. "Agricultural Conditions in the Northern Colonies Before the Revolution," Journal of Economic History, XIII (Summer 1953).

Sachs, William S. and Hoogenboom, Ari. The Enterprising Colonials. Chicago: Argonaut, Inc., Publishers, 1969.

Savelle, Max. The Foundation of American Civilization. New York: Holt, Rinehart & Winston, 1962.

Shepherd, James E., and Walton, Gary M. Shipping, Maritime Trade, and Economic Development. Cambridge: Cambridge University Press, 1972.

_____. "Trade Distribution, andEconomic Growth in Colonial America," Journal of Economic History, XXXII (March, 1972).

Taylor, George Rogers. American Economic Growth Before 1840: An Exploratory Essay." Journal of Economic History, XXIV (Dec., 1964).

Walton, Gary. "Sources of Productivity Change in American Colonial Shipping 1675-1775," Economic History Review, XX, 2nd Series (April, 1967).

Weeden, William B. Economic and Social History of New England 1620-1789, 2 Vols. New York: Hillary House Publishers, Ltd., 1963.

Wright, Harry Andrew. "The Technique of Seventeenth-Century Indian-Land Purchases." Essex Institute Historical Collections, LXXVII (1941).

Dissertations in American Economic History

An Arno Press Collection

Adams, Donald R., Jr. **Wage Rates in Philadelphia, 1790-1830.** (Doctoral Dissertation, University of Pennsylvania, 1967). 1975

Aldrich, Terry Mark. **Rates of Return on Investment in Technical Education in the Ante-Bellum American Economy.** (Doctoral Dissertation, The University of Texas at Austin, 1969). 1975

Anderson, Terry Lee. **The Economic Growth of Seventeenth Century New England:** A Measurement of Regional Income. (Doctoral Dissertation, University of Washington, 1972). 1975

Bean, Richard Nelson. **The British Trans-Atlantic Slave Trade, 1650-1775.** (Doctoral Dissertation, University of Washington, 1971). 1975

Brock, Leslie V. **The Currency of the American Colonies, 1700-1764:** A Study in Colonial Finance and Imperial Relations. (Doctoral Dissertation, University of Michigan, 1941). 1975

Ellsworth, Lucius F. **Craft to National Industry in the Nineteenth Century:** A Case Study of the Transformation of the New York State Tanning Industry. (Doctoral Dissertation, University of Delaware, 1971). 1975

Fleisig, Heywood W. **Long Term Capital Flows and the Great Depression:** The Role of the United States, 1927-1933. (Doctoral Dissertation, Yale University, 1969). 1975

Foust, James D. **The Yeoman Farmer and Westward Expansion of U. S. Cotton Production.** (Doctoral Dissertation, University of North Carolina at Chapel Hill, 1968). 1975

Golden, James Reed. **Investment Behavior By United States Railroads, 1870-1914.** (Doctoral Thesis, Harvard University, 1971). 1975

Hill, Peter Jensen. **The Economic Impact of Immigration into the United States.** (Doctoral Dissertation, The University of Chicago, 1970). 1975

Klingaman, David C. **Colonial Virginia's Coastwise and Grain Trade.** (Doctoral Dissertation, University of Virginia, 1967). 1975

Lang, Edith Mae. **The Effects of Net Interregional Migration on Agricultural Income Growth:** The United States, 1850-1860. (Doctoral Thesis, The University of Rochester, 1971). 1975

Lindley, Lester G. **The Constitution Faces Technology:** The Relationship of the National Government to the Telegraph, 1866-1884. (Doctoral Thesis, Rice University, 1971). 1975

Lorant, John H[erman]. **The Role of Capital-Improving Innovations in American Manufacturing During the 1920's.** (Doctoral Thesis, Columbia University, 1966). 1975

Mishkin, David Joel. **The American Colonial Wine Industry:** An Economic Interpretation, Volumes I and II. (Doctoral Thesis, University of Illinois, 1966). 1975

Oates, Mary J. **The Role of the Cotton Textile Industry in the Economic Development of the American Southeast:** 1900-1940. (Doctoral Dissertation, Yale University, 1969). 1975

Passell, Peter. **Essays in the Economics of Nineteenth Century American Land Policy.** (Doctoral Dissertation, Yale University, 1970). 1975

Pope, Clayne L. **The Impact of the Ante-Bellum Tariff on Income Distribution.** (Doctoral Dissertation, The University of Chicago, 1972). 1975

Poulson, Barry Warren. **Value Added in Manufacturing, Mining, and Agriculture in the American Economy From 1809 To 1839.** (Doctoral Dissertation, The Ohio State University, 1965). 1975

Rockoff, Hugh. **The Free Banking Era: A Re-Examination.** (Doctoral Dissertation, The University of Chicago, 1972). 1975

Schumacher, Max George. **The Northern Farmer and His Markets During the Late Colonial Period.** (Doctoral Dissertation, University of California at Berkeley, 1948). 1975

Seagrave, Charles Edwin. **The Southern Negro Agricultural Worker:** 1850-1870. (Doctoral Dissertation, Stanford University, 1971). 1975

Solmon, Lewis C. **Capital Formation by Expenditures on Formal Education, 1880 and 1890.** (Doctoral Dissertation, The University of Chicago, 1968). 1975

Swan, Dale Evans. **The Structure and Profitability of the Antebellum Rice Industry:** 1859. (Doctoral Dissertation, University of North Carolina at Chapel Hill, 1972). 1975

Sylla, Richard Eugene. **The American Capital Market, 1846-1914:** A Study of the Effects of Public Policy on Economic Development. (Doctoral Thesis, Harvard University, 1968) 1975

Uselding, Paul John. **Studies in the Technological Development of the American Economy During the First Half of the Nineteenth Century.** (Doctoral Dissertation, Northwestern University, 1970) 1975

Walsh, William D[avid]. **The Diffusion of Technological Change in the Pennsylvania Pig Iron Industry, 1850-1870.** (Doctoral Dissertation, Yale University, 1967). 1975

Weiss, Thomas Joseph. **The Service Sector in the United States, 1839 Through 1899.** (Doctoral Thesis, University of North Carolina at Chapel Hill, 1967). 1975

Zevin, Robert Brooke. **The Growth of Manufacturing in Early Nineteenth Century New England.** 1975